FIVE TELEVISION PLAYS

FIVE TELEVISION PLAYS

A Waitress in Yellowstone
or *Always Tell the Truth*

Bradford

The Museum of Science and Industry Story

A Wasted Weekend

We Will Take You There

DAVID MAMET

GROVE WEIDENFELD
New York

Published by Grove Weidenfeld
A division of Wheatland Corporation
841 Broadway
New York, NY 10003-4793

Published in Canada by General Publishing Company, Ltd.

Library of Congress Cataloging-in-Publication Data

Mamet, David.
[Plays.   Selections]
Five television plays / David Mamet.—1st ed.
p.   cm.
Contents: A waitress in Yellowstone—Bradford—The Museum of
Science and Industry story—A wasted weekend—We will take you there.
1. Television plays, American.   I. Title.
PS3563.A4345A6   1990
812'.54—dc20   89-25661
                                                              CIP
ISBN 0-8021-3171-9

Printed on acid-free paper

Designed by Irving Perkins Associates

First Edition 1990

1   2   3   4   5   6   7   8   9   10

Contents

Introduction

I GREW UP in the Golden Age of Television. I remember nightly and weekly exuberance and excellence: "Your Show of Shows," "Gunsmoke," "Medic," "Have Gun Will Travel," "Twilight Zone," "The Jackie Gleason Show," et cetera. Reviewing these shows after twenty or thirty years is instructive and sobering—they stand the test of time—not that each show is a comic or dramatic masterpiece, but *many* are, and the bulk of the entertainment is well designed, and executed with spirit.

These shows of the fifties and many of the sixties are, and it is in this that they differ from today's television, honestly done. They are, in the main, honest attempts to dramatize, to cheer, to divert, to entertain. It was inevitable that the Bad Money drive out the good, that a drama broken every eight minutes by an advertisement the revenue from which funded the drama should eventually become a teaser for that upcoming advertisement. It was inevitable that the primacy of the ad revenues would bring about a whorehouse mentality in the Television Industry: "Give 'em as little as you can, and get 'em out of here as soon as possible"; and that the pimps and hucksters would not only achieve dominance over, but eventually eliminate those drawn to television as a new theatrical form.

Television executives are the worst people I have ever met in my life. Their conversations with me over the years have always started, "Mr. Mamet, we are so honored that you would even *consider* writing for television"; for which unsolicited and totally false asseveration they then proceeded to make me pay at length.

I would love to write for television. I love the form. I grew up with it. As a child I watched television ten hours a day. It was my dramatic training. I can imagine no greater fun than having my own television show and writing and directing for the same actors and characters every week. I was in at the conclusion of the "Hill Street Blues" series and had the time of my life. The "Hill Street" script, *A Wasted Weekend,* here included, is the only piece of television writing I ever did which got made.

Lovely exciting medium. What a shame.

Sour grapes? Most certainly. As I said, I love the form, and I wish I could have played along.

David Mamet
1988

A Waitress in Yellowstone
or *Always Tell the Truth*

Dramatis Personae

RANGER
WAITRESS
OLD MAN (OLD COUPLE)
WINNIE MAGEE
CONGRESSMAN JOHN LARUE
BOSS
COP
DOUG MAGEE, WINNIE'S SON (AGE 10)
RADIO ANNOUNCER (VOICE OVER ONLY)
POLICEMAN
SECOND POLICEMAN
JUDGE
BAILIFF
LAWYER FOR CONGRESSMAN
CONVICT (FEMALE)
GUARD
BUS DRIVER
STATE TROOPER
SECOND STATE TROOPER
RALPH BLUM (THE MAGIC WOODSMAN)

Narrator takes stage. Dressed as park ranger.

RANGER: Winnie was a waitress. She worked for tips. Here is a tip: a
bad situation generally grows worse.

Things which can get no worse improve. There are exceptions: here is
not one. Winnie caught a guy lifting a tip off of her table. Told him
"who do you think you are?" and she read him out to the onlooking
crowd, what sort of you-fill-in-the-blank that he *was* . . . which
he was.

It turns out this man was a congressman. In an election year. He had
to keep a shining image in the public eye, which is exactly where he
kept it.

Would have been better off to be what he wished to seem, but barring
that he took the secondary course, lived like a thief and made the
Public Pay.

Winnie and her son Doug. Had planned a trip to Yellowstone. To
celebrate his Tenth Birthday. He'd, as you might imagine, looked
forward to that trip all year. And it was the object of much of their
talk and much of their joint happiness.

At the restaurant.

WAITRESS: Hey, Winnie, quit dreaming, table number three wants
the check!

(OLD COUPLE.)

OLD MAN: Could I have the check, please.

WINNIE: Here you are.

OLD MAN: Thank you. See you tomorrow, Winnie . . .

WINNIE: No you won't, sir. Tomorrow my boy and I leave for our vacation. I'll see you in two weeks.

OLD MAN: Where are you going?

WINNIE: Yellowstone Park.

OLD MAN: That's right, you told me. Here's a little extra, you have a fine trip.

(*The* OLD COUPLE *starts up to leave.*)

WINNIE: That's *very* generous of you, sir . . . thank you . . . (*Before she can gather the money, etc., she is called to another table.*)

CONGRESSMAN: Miss!

WINNIE (*to* OLD MAN): Thank you very much.

CONGRESSMAN: Miss!

WINNIE: I'm coming! (*To* CONGRESSMAN:) Yes, sir?

CONGRESSMAN (*of check*): What is the meaning of this?

WINNIE (*checking bill*): Ninety-five cents, for a substitution. You had beans instead of the creamed spinach.

CONGRESSMAN: You never told me that.

WINNIE: Yes, sir, I did.

CONGRESSMAN: You certainly did *not*. You did *not* tell me that.

WINNIE: Yes, sir, I am certain, you said "I'll have the Special." Look: It's not important. If you take the check to the boss, I'm sure that he'll . . .

CONGRESSMAN: Well, that's not the point, is it? The point is that you never *told* me . . .

WINNIE: Well, if that's true, I'm sorry, sir.

CONGRESSMAN: No: *say* you never told me . . .

WINNIE: Excuse me . . .

CONGRESSMAN: You owe me an apology.

WINNIE: I think that I apologized, excuse me . . . (*She walks away. To another* WAITRESS:) Some people have too much salt in their diet . . . (*To* CONGRESSMAN:) WAIT A SECOND WAIT A SECOND WAIT A SECOND: *WAIT* A SECOND THERE!

(*She walks back to his table, which he has gotten up from. He is standing near the table vacated by the* OLD COUPLE. *To* CONGRESSMAN:)

You wanna put something back? (*Pause.*) You wanna put something back, or you want me to call the police.

CONGRESSMAN: I don't know what you're talking about.

WINNIE: I'm talking about you just lifted my tip off of that table. Now: you put it back or I call the cops.

CONGRESSMAN: You're saying . . . (*Pause.*) You're saying I did whhh . . . ? Get out of my way. (*Tries to push past her.*)

WINNIE: In a pig's *eye* I will. Somebody call the cops! Somebody call the cops, this guy took my tip off the . . . (*To* CONGRESSMAN:) You aren't going anywhere!

BOSS: What's the trouble?

WINNIE: This guy took my tip off the table.

CONGRESSMAN: Lady, you're in a world of trouble here.

WINNIE: Well, we're just going to see . . .

COP: What seems to be the trouble?

WINNIE: This guy lifted my tip off the table.

CONGRESSMAN: Not only is it not true, but I want to tell you you've just caused yourself a lot of pain. What's your name, Officer? I'm John Larue, I am the congressman for this district, and this deranged and sick individual has just slandered me. Pick her *tip* off the table? You know WHO I *AM*???

(*The* CONGRESSMAN *sings about the exalted position he enjoys. He finishes singing.*)

CONGRESSMAN: Now: I'll give you one last chance to retract what you said and take back your vicious lie, or you're going to wish you never were born.

WINNIE: Well, to wish you never were born you have to be born. Which gives you the option, and I think I'll stick with the truth. You should be ashamed of yourself. Good-bye.

(*The* COP *takes the* CONGRESSMAN *away.*)

WINNIE: What kind of a world is it? That guy should be setting an example . . .

(WINNIE *and the assembled* CUSTOMERS *sing "What Kind of a World Is It?" peppering the song with examples from their own lives. The second verse is: "On the Other Hand," where* WINNIE *sings about some of the good things which may be had simply in life, in her case, the trip with her son to Yellowstone Park.*
As the clock strikes twelve she sings "My Day Is Done, and I'm Going on Vacation," and leaves the restaurant. She walks home.)

WINNIE: Look at the stars, what a beautiful night it is. Always various. (*She walks into her house.*) Look at my son, isn't he gorgeous. And now we have all this vacation time to be alone together. All the rest is basically illusion.

RANGER: And so she fell asleep, and she and her son dreamed the same dream. In which they were in Yellowstone Park, high upon a ridge, upon a summit, looking down, and they saw mountain sheep, and they saw deer, and when the rain came unexpectedly they made a shelter from a fallen tree. And as in the wild of sleep and as in the wild of the forest their cares fell away. And when Winnie awoke, she saw her son, already dressed, sitting at the breakfast table, and he had made her a cup of tea.

(*N.B. They are both dressed in full camp regalia.*)

WINNIE: Good morning. What are you doing up so early?

DOUG: Oh, I couldn't sleep.

WINNIE: Why? You worried about school, shouldn't you be off to school?

DOUG: Well, I thought I wouldn't go to school today?

WINNIE: Wouldn't go to school? Why, of course, you have to go to school today, why wouldn't you?

DOUG: 'CAUSE WE'RE GOING TO YELLOWSTONE PARK!!!!!

(*They jump up and down and sing a song about how they must make sure they've taken the right things. They sing about the contents of a rucksack, and emergency gear, which they inspect on each other's person. This gear includes: waxed matches in a waterproof container {several containers secreted in various parts of the clothing and generally high up to keep them dry should one fall into waist-high water}, a compass, a spare compass, a topographic map of the area to be camped in. A candle for helping to light fires, needle and thread, steel wool which, though it is not generally known, is, in its superfine variety, great tinder and can just be wrung out when wet, extra clothing, rain gear, pencil and paper, fishing line and hook, bandages, whistle, etc. They finish the song, and, having checked each other out, decide that they are ready to proceed to the bus, which they have ten minutes to catch. In deciding which coat to wear, they turn on the radio to catch a weather report.*)

DOUG: I can't believe we're really going.

WINNIE: Have I ever lied to you?

DOUG: No!

WINNIE: Well, then, there you are.

RADIO ANNOUNCER (*voice over*): In other news, Congressman John Larue, up for reelection, yesterday was accosted for the misdemeanor of Attempting to Defraud of Services, or, to put it simply, a waitress at a restaurant he frequents, accused the Congressman of lifting her tip off her table.

WINNIE: . . . come on, let's get out of here . . .

CONGRESSMAN (*voice over*): You know, it's easy to accuse, and, I think by far the simplest thing would be to let this sick accusation pass, and go my way, but there comes a time . . .

WINNIE: Turn that creep off, let's go to the *country* . . .

DOUG (*turns off radio*): What'd he do?

WINNIE: The creep. Lifted a tip off of a waitress's table. Can you believe that?

DOUG (*opening door*): What a life.

WINNIE: On to the Wilds!

(*In the door are two burly plainclothes* POLICEMEN.)

POLICEMAN: Winnie Magee?

WINNIE: I . . . uh, what is it?

POLICEMAN: Are you Ms. Winnie Magee?

WINNIE: I can't talk to you now, we have to catch a bus.

POLICEMAN: ARE YOU WIN . . . ?

WINNIE: Yes, but I can't talk . . .

POLICEMAN (*simultaneously with "talk"*): You're under arrest. Would you come with us, please?

WINNIE: I . . .

DOUG: Wait, you can't, what's this all . . . ?

POLICEMAN: Slander, Malicious Mischief, Defamation of Character, would you please . . . ?

WINNIE: Who, what . . . ?

DOUG: What are you doing to my mother?

SECOND POLICEMAN: She insulted a congressman, kid.

WINNIE: But we . . . we just have ten minutes to catch the *bus* . . .

(*They are in a court of law.*)

And we're going to Yellowstone P . . . what is this, what's going on here . . . ?

JUDGE: You are accused of wantonly, maliciously, and with malice aforethought having verbally assaulted, insulted, and impugned the character of one John Larue, Congressman for the Seventh District of . . .

WINNIE: HOLD ON A SECOND. I insulted wh . . . ?

JUDGE: You have no voice in this court, would you please, who is your counsel?

WINNIE: Say that again?

BAILIFF: Who's your lawyer?

WINNIE: I don't have a lawyer, why should . . . What's going on here? (*Pause.*) Come on, I have to catch a *bus. (Pause.*)

JUDGE: You are accused by the Congressman here (CONGRESSMAN

stands) of, in simple terms, of lying about him in such a way as to damage his reputation.

WINNIE: Ah.

JUDGE: When you said that he stole your tip.

WINNIE: He *did* steal my tip.

JUDGE: The court will now appoint you a lawyer.

WINNIE: I don't need a lawyer, I don't *want* one. Let's settle this here and now, 'cause I'm on my vacation time, alright? You tell me how you want to do this, and let's get this done.

JUDGE: You wish to act as your own lawyer?

WINNIE: That's . . . okay. (*Pause.*) Okay.

JUDGE: You're making a mistake.

WINNIE: I've made them before. Nothing to be scared of, now: what is the thing?

DOUG: Mom, what's going on . . . ?

(WINNIE *and* DOUG *hold a whispered consultation while the* BAILIFF *and the* JUDGE *sing about the charge and the procedure in this case. They are joined by the* LAWYER *for the* CONGRESSMAN *and the* CONGRESSMAN, *who sing about her heinous behavior and the grave damage that has been done. They stop. Pause.*)

WINNIE: Now what?

JUDGE: You may present your case.

WINNIE: It's my turn to speak?

JUDGE: Yes.

WINNIE (*sings*):
    Let me preface my remarks by saying
    that I have to catch a bus
    Because I am enroute to Yellowstone Park
    Where, my son and I are taking
    a long-planned vacation
    In the wilds of this great land.
    I am a simple kind of gal which is to say
    I'm just as complex as the rest of us here but
    there are some basic things that I believe in
    one of which is
    that we are entitled to a just pay
    for the work that we do
    in my case a waitress
    which is to say that I work for tips.
    Okay?
    My salary is directly tied to this one thing:
    my ability to *please,* which is to say, to make comfortable
    the *patrons* of my restaurant, who have come out to eat.
    The first rule of which is:
    THE CUSTOMER IS ALWAYS RIGHT.
    Which rule I do adhere to.
    IN THIS CASE HOWEVER. ONE:
    The man performed a criminal act . . .

CONGRESSMAN: . . . I DID NOT.

WINNIE: AND I asked him . . .

LAWYER: What was that act?

WINNIE: He stole my tip.

LAWYER: I rest my case.

WINNIE: I asked him to replace it. He did not, and two: I called upon the customers to help me out. That's the beginning and the end, and that is what occurred. Now; are we free to leave?

DOUG: Can we go now?

(*End of song.*)

JUDGE: Can you prove that he took your tip?

WINNIE: No.

JUDGE: You can not?

WINNIE: No. The only proof is that I saw him.

JUDGE: We will now consider this case.

DOUG: Mom, do we have time to make the bus . . . ?

WINNIE (*simultaneously with "bus"*): Just barely. If he does this quick.

JUDGE: Here are my feelings: this has gotten out of hand. I think it can be settled quickly. (*Pause.*) As we all have better things to do. (*Pause.*) I think that a simple apology will suffice.

WINNIE: I'll accept that. Your Honor. I notice that you didn't say that he had to give back my tip. There is a principle involved, but I am willing to forget that, in the interest of getting out of town . . . (*To* DOUG, *as she checks her watch:*) Okay, let's go, we can just make it . . . (*They walk toward the courtroom doors carrying their rucksacks.*) And I will waive that principle and accept the Congressman's sincere apology. Also, he has to say he'll never do it again.

JUDGE: You misunderstand me. *You'll* have to apologize to *him*.

(*Pause.*)

WINNIE: I . . . *what?*

JUDGE: *You* will have to . . .

WINNIE: *I* . . . ?

JUDGE: Apologize to the Congressman.

(*Pause.*)

WINNIE: For *what?*

JUDGE: For maligning his reputation.

WINNIE: HE STOLE MY *TIP.*

JUDGE: We have no way of knowing *what* he might have done, except your word. His reputation, which is a weighty thing, is at stake, and rather than *prolong* this, and to allow you to catch your bus, if you will just state that you . . . *could* have made a mistake . . .

LAWYER: I OBJECT.

JUDGE: Excuse me: if you will just say that you *could* have made a mistake, this case will be closed and you can go to Yellowstone.

(*Pause.*)

WINNIE: You want me to say he didn't steal my tip. (*Pause.*) I do that and we can go.

JUDGE: Yes.

WINNIE: What if I don't say that?

JUDGE: You will go to jail.

WINNIE: Hmm.

(*Pause.*)

JUDGE: The choice is yours. What do you choose to do? And I would remind you that you have but five minutes to catch your bus.

WINNIE: Well. This would seem to be the crux of the whole matter here.

RANGER: I would say so.

WINNIE (*to* DOUG): Whaddya think, kid? This guy stole my tip, and if I lie about it we can go free, if not . . . it's, it's your *trip,* you tell mmm . . . naa, that's *ridiculous.* What am I going to do? Teach my kid his mom's a liar for the sake of *expediency?*

LAWYER: He wants to go camping.

WINNIE: So he won't go camping. That's not under my control, and I never promised him that I was *superman,* all that I told him was I'd tell the truth.

JUDGE: And so?

WINNIE: Take me to jail and be damned with you. He stole my tip. (*She is led from the courtroom, amidst catcalls.*)

CONGRESSMAN: What kind of a mother are you?

LAWYER: You're going to be a convict . . .

WINNIE: Hey, I'd rather be me than *you*.

BAILIFF: You promised the child you'd take him camping.

DOUG: Mama!

WINNIE: Well, there's nothing we can do about it . . .

RANGER: And so Winnie was taken to the jail, and they took her picture and her fingerprints, and they gave her a uniform and put her in a cell.

(*In the cell. With another* CONVICT.)

CONVICT: You want to play gin?

WINNIE: Don't bother me.

RANGER: And she was full of longing for her son, whom she missed. And she worried about him. And she thought about him.

(WINNIE *sings a song about how incredibly difficult it is to bring up children. And how hard it is to live your life according to first principles. The song ends.*)

CONVICT: The first night is the hardest.

WINNIE: I'm sure that's true.

CONVICT: It *is* true. (*Pause.*) How long are you in for?

WINNIE: I don't know. 'Til I apologize. (*Sighs.*) And we were supposed to be camped out beneath the stars. (*Pause.*) How long are *you* in for?

CONVICT: Can you keep a secret?

WINNIE: No. (*Pause.*)

CONVICT: What's *that* supposed to mean?

WINNIE: Nobody can keep a secret. If you don't want me to know your business don't tell it to me.

CONVICT: We're breaking out.

WINNIE: What does that mean?

CONVICT: We're breaking out of jail tonight.

WINNIE: Swell.

(*There is a huge explosion, and the prison wall collapses. All the* CONVICTS *run. She finds herself among them.*)

GUARD: Stop! Stop!

WINNIE: Look, I just, I was just sitting in my *cell* . . .

(*The* GUARD *fires at her.*)

WINNIE: Oh gosh . . . ! (*She runs.*)

RANGER: And so Winnie ran from the prison, along with the other convicts. And she wandered in the dark corners of the streets. And she found herself at home.

(*Outside her apartment. Her son, listening to the radio.*)

ANNOUNCER (*voice over*): And now a medley of Songs That You Love To Dream Along With. From the Fantasy Ballroom.

(*Old-time music begins to play.* WINNIE *goes inside.*)

DOUG: Mama! (*They embrace.*) Mama! I knew that you'd come home. I knew that you'd come home!!!

WINNIE: How are you, Sweetie?

DOUG: I knew that you'd come back. I knew they'd let you out. So we could go *camping*.

WINNIE: Doug, *look:* I, uh . . . I don't think we can . . .

ANNOUNCER (*voice over*): We interrupt this program to bring you a special report. Inmates from the Women's Correctional Institute escaped tonight in a mass breakout, wounding five guards in the attempt. Considered armed and dangerous, be on the lookout for . . .

(*She turns off the radio.*)

WINNIE (*pause*): Um . . .

DOUG: I'll just get my pack. (*He checks bus schedule.*) And we can catch a bus at . . .

WINNIE: . . . Doug . . .

DOUG: We can catch the one forty-five A.M. bus. And tomorrow! . . . Tomorrow . . . that's right: Yellowstone P . . .

WINNIE: Doug . . . (*Pause.*) Hm. Get your pack.

RANGER: They disguised themselves, and got on the bus bound for Yellowstone.

(*On the bus. In wigs, and so on.*)

DOUG: Will everything be alright?

WINNIE: Everything is never alright; but the thing of it is you never have to worry about "everything." And, for the moment, what we're going to do is just go camping. Now you go to sleep.

(*He goes to sleep, as she sings him a song about Yellowstone, a lullaby, featuring the admonition not to feed the bears, and to look out not to miss Old Faithful.*)

RANGER: The bus sped West, and they fell asleep rocked to the rhythm of the bus.

(WINNIE *is suddenly awake. To* BUS DRIVER.)

WINNIE: Why are we slowing down?

DRIVER: There's something up ahead. It's a roadblock.

(*The lights come on in the bus.* STATE TROOPERS *enter.*)

TROOPER: Would everyone please keep their seats.

(*They start down the aisle, looking at a picture and at the passengers.*)

DRIVER: What's the trouble?

TROOPER: We're looking for some Escaped Convicts . . .

DOUG: What are we going to do?

WINNIE: Be calm.

DOUG: How can I, how can I be calm? They're going to Take you Away.

WINNIE: Just, Sweetie, just be . . . just, whatever I say, you pretend you're asleep.

TROOPER (*to* WINNIE): What is your name?

DOUG: She's You Don't Want Her. She isn't anybody. Don't . . . don't take her. Mama. Come on. Let's Run!

WINNIE: Officer, I . . .

DOUG: She's not the one you want . . . Come ON!

RANGER: He and his mother escaped through a back window of the bus. And they ran into the woods.

DOUG: Keep running . . .

WINNIE (*sighs*): Oh, my god . . .

DOUG: No, all we have to do is just keep running. They won't . . . they won't find us . . .

WINNIE: Alright.

DOUG: Don't go back. You can't go back. They'll put you back in Prison.

WINNIE: Alright.

RANGER: In the deep dark they became lost. In the woods.

WINNIE: Are you alright?

DOUG: I'm cold.

WINNIE (*of compass*): We'll just keep walking North. We're going to find a road.

DOUG: How do you know?

WINNIE: Because I have the compass and I have a map.

DOUG: How do you know that there *is* a road?

WINNIE: Because I see it on the map.

DOUG: What will we do when we find it?

WINNIE: Give ourselves up, because you're cold, and you should be warm, and sleep. And we can't run forever. And that's what we're going to do.

DOUG: We're going the wrong way. We *passed* this way before.

WINNIE: No. We didn't.

DOUG: How do you know?

WINNIE: Because I have my compass.

DOUG: I don't think it's working. Yes it is. We'll trust it now. And everything will be alright.

WINNIE: Now; for a moment. What's the first thing that you do if you get scared and you're lost in the woods?

DOUG: I don't know.

WINNIE: Yes. You do. You Sit Down and Think. (*Pause.*) Now we'll sit down a moment.

(*They sit.* WINNIE *sings: "Just Because You're Lost Don't Think Your Compass Is Broken." She sings: "We Must Abide, in Moments of Stress, by Those Things We Have, in Moments of Peace, Decided Are Correct." She finishes singing.*)

Now, let's go on, and soon we'll find the road, and then you'll be warm.

DOUG: Look!

WINNIE: What is it?

DOUG: A light!

RANGER: They walked in the forest to a little hut made out of wood. A sign over the door said "Ralph Blum."

WINNIE: Ralph Blum.

DOUG: Who is that?

WINNIE: I don't know, but I hope that he'll help.

(*She knocks on the door. Pause. She knocks again. Pause.*)

DOUG: Let's go in.

(WINNIE *tries the door.*)

WINNIE: It's locked. Well, we're going to get you warm. We'll break a window.

(*They start around the side of the cabin, the door opens.*)

RALPH: Who are you?

WINNIE: May we come in? My son is . . .

RALPH: Why didn't you come to the door?

WINNIE: We *did* come to the door. We knocked and knocked and . . .

RALPH: I didn't hear you. Come in.

(*They go into the cabin.*)

RALPH: The boy's cold? Let's get him something to eat. Here. Put on those warm clothes and I'll put the bed by the fire.

WINNIE: Thank you.

RALPH: What?

WINNIE: Thank you.

RALPH: Not at all.

RANGER: So they sat around the fire and the man gave them soup.

RALPH: Now, you two should go to bed, because you look like you could use the rest. You go to sleep, now.

WINNIE: I don't think that I can sleep.

RALPH: You sleep, and everything will look brighter in the morning, whatever it is.

WINNIE: I don't think so.

(*Pause.*)

RALPH: Is there anything that I can help you with?

WINNIE: Thank you, you're very kind, I don't see how you can.

RALPH: You never know. Did you know that? That's one of the true things. You never know.

WINNIE: I'm sure you're right.

RALPH: What?

WINNIE: I said I'm sure you're right.

RALPH: I am right. Lived in the forest all my life. You think that's crazy?

WINNIE: Not at all. Quite the contrary.

RALPH: Eh?

WINNIE: I think that's the best place one could live.

RALPH: You *do?*

WINNIE: Yes.

RALPH: Huh. Huh. Huh. (*Pause.*) Well, I'm going to tell you what: Us Outdoorsmen have got to help each other. Don't you think? (*Pause.*) Don't you think?

WINNIE: Mm. Yes.

RALPH: Well, we *do.* And I'm going to help *you.* I don't know what your *problems* are, 'n' it's none of my business . . .

WINNIE: My problems are I have to go to jail and be separated from my son tomorrow.

RALPH: Then I'm going to help you.

WINNIE: How?

(*Pause.*)

RALPH: Can you keep a secret?

WINNIE: If it will help me and my son.

RALPH: It will.

WINNIE: Then I'll keep a secret.

RALPH: You give me your solemn oath?

WINNIE: I do.

RALPH: Alright. (*Pause.*) I am the Magic Woodsman. (*Pause.*) I have the Power to grant Wishes of the Heart.

(*He sings the "Song of the Magic Woodsman." He finishes. Pause.*)

And now you have two wishes. Anything your Heart Desires.

(*Pause.*)

WINNIE: I can wish for anything?

RALPH: Yup. And it will be granted.

(*Pause.*)

WINNIE: Is that true?

RALPH: Yes. It is.

(*Pause.*)

WINNIE: Thank you.

RALPH: What?

WINNIE: Thank you.

RALPH: That is alright. Now, you take your time, and whatever you . . .

WINNIE: I don't have to take time. I am going to wish . . .

RALPH: Oh, oh, oh. I forgot: (*pause*) First you have to guess my name. Nothing to it. (*Pause.*) You have to guess my name and then I grant your wishes. Understand?

WINNIE: Yes.

RALPH: Think that you can do it?

WINNIE: Yes.

RALPH: Alright, then. Now: what are your wishes?

WINNIE (*pause*): I wish that everything was just the way it was before the congressman came in the restaurant . . .

RALPH: . . . alright . . .

WINNIE: And I wish my son and I were in Yellowstone Park. (*Pause.*)

RALPH: Good. You tell me my name your wishes shall be granted.

WINNIE: Your name is Ralph Blum. (*Pause.*)

RALPH: I'm very sorry, Miss.

WINNIE: That's not your name?

RALPH: I'm very sorry. (*Pause.*) I'm very sorry.

WINNIE: Do I get another chance?

RALPH: No. It is not within my power. (*Pause.*) I'm very sorry. (*Pause.*) I . . . you and the boy. Feel free to stay here tonight. I, I'm sure everything will, will look brighter in the morning. (*Pause.*) I hope that everything works out. I'm very sorry.

(*The* MAGIC WOODSMAN *leaves the cabin.* WINNIE *waits. Sits down at the table, smokes a cigarette.*)

RANGER: The false dawn came, that time before the dawn, and, after it, the dawn, and Winnie sat at the table smoking her cigarette while her son slept.

(WINNIE *sings a song of remorse, how, standing on principle, she has sacrificed the well-being of her child. She finishes.* DOUG *wakes up.*)

DOUG: Where are we . . . ?

WINNIE: Come on. Get up, Sweetheart, we . . .

DOUG: What's that . . . ?

RANGER: They heard the baying of dogs. Drawing closer.

WINNIE: They're coming to get us.

(*Through a megaphone we hear a* TROOPER.)

TROOPER: We know you're in there . . .

SECOND TROOPER: Be careful, she's dangerous.

TROOPER: You have one minute to come out, you and the boy . . .

DOUG: What are we going to do?

WINNIE: I have to give myself up . . .

DOUG: No! What will they do to . . .

WINNIE: I'm sure everything will be al . . .

TROOPER: Alright, we're coming in . . .

WINNIE (*she embraces* DOUG): Sweetheart, I'm sure that everything will be al . . .

(*The door opens. She shields* DOUG. *It is* RALPH BLUM.)

RALPH: Wait a second. Did you say "Ralph *Blum*"?

WINNIE: What?

RALPH: Did you say "Ralph *Blum*"? My *name?*

WINNIE: Yes.

RALPH: You *did*.

WINNIE: Yes.

RALPH: Cause, that *is* my name. It's on, you know, it's on a sign right outside the *door.*

WINNIE: I, I, I *know.*

RALPH: What?

WINNIE: I said that I *know*.

RALPH: I thought you said "Brown." But you said "Ralph *Blum*."

WINNIE: Yes.

RALPH: Word of honor?

WINNIE: Yes.

RALPH: Well, then you get your *wish!* *I'm* sorry . . . such a silly . . . I don't *hear* so . . .

(*They are transported.* WINNIE *is back in the restaurant with the* CON-GRESSMAN.)

RANGER: And they were magically transported back in time. To the time before she saw the congressman take the tip from the table.

(*At the restaurant.*)

CONGRESSMAN: Miss.

WINNIE: Yes, sir, I'm coming.

CONGRESSMAN (*of check*): What is this? Ninety-five cents for a substitution?

WINNIE: You had beans instead of the creamed spinach.

CONGRESSMAN: I'm not going to pay it.

WINNIE: Then I will pay it for you. 'Cause I bet you've had a hard day.

CONGRESSMAN: Uh. You will?

WINNIE: Yes.

CONGRESSMAN: That's, uh, you know, it's not the money, it's the principle of the thing.

WINNIE: I know that it is.

CONGRESSMAN: That's very kind of you.

WINNIE: Just Pass it On.

(*Another* WAITRESS *and she talk.*)

WAITRESS: That fellow giving you a hard time?

WINNIE: Well, you know, it takes all kinds.

WAITRESS: Hey: your vacation starts tomorrow.

WINNIE: You bet. Me and my Son are going to Yellowstone.

WAITRESS: I bet that you wish you were there right now.

WINNIE: I surely do.

RANGER: And they were all instantly transported to Yellowstone Park, the Congressman, the Judge, the Bailiff, the Guards and the Prisoners, and Winnie and her Son. For two weeks of life in the Great Outdoors.

They all sing a chorale. To wit:

> Always tell the truth.
> Never insult a congressman.
> Don't go to court without a lawyer.
> Be calm at Roadblocks.
> Do not feed the bears.

Bradford

Dramatis Personae

FADE IN.
EXTERIOR: MAIN STREET, BRADFORD, A SMALL NEW EN-
GLAND TOWN.

*Pan past several firemen working in the ruins of a burnt, still smoldering
building, across the street to the facade of an old diner, "The Coffeecorner."*

(*ANGLE INTERIOR: THE COFFEECORNER. Businessmen in shirt-
sleeves, in the bay window, looking out at the burnt building.*)

BUSINESSMAN: . . . gonna cost *someone* couple bucks, put that building back up.

SECOND BUSINESSMAN: The question is, but who.

BUSINESSMAN: *Another* question: Who did what?

SECOND BUSINESSMAN: Well, that's *always* the issue, isn't it . . . ?

(*An old* WAITRESS *tops up their coffee. Camera pans with the* WAITRESS,
back behind the counter.)

WAITRESS: . . . top it up, Harry?

HARRY: Thank you very much. (*He addresses the man to his right:*) All
I'm saying, you get people down the Capital, telling *other* people how
to live their lives, and got no *notion* how those people live, then, yes,
then people lose their respect for the Institution.

(*The* WAITRESS *takes a pot of coffee. Camera follows her down to the far end of the counter, past a* FARMER.)

FARMER: What they talking about down there?

WAITRESS: Oh, they're arguing about the *Doe* season . . .

FARMER: Jimmy! Whyn't you come up with a new subject, talk about the *weather,* some damn thing.

BUSINESSMAN: Weather's *changing* all the time, you talk about the *weather,* you never know where you stand . . .

(*Camera follows her down to* PRICE, *a man around forty, in a corduroy sportscoat, plain shirt, and a tie. He is looking at a road map.*)

WAITRESS: More coffee . . . ?

PRICE: Yes. Thank you.

WAITRESS: 'Nother order toast?

PRICE (*checks his watch*): No, thank you. I don't have time.

BUSINESSMAN (*offstage*): Yes, I can attest to the *usefulness* of passing *laws,* but I can't see laws 'bout something none of your concern.

PRICE (*to the* WAITRESS. *He points to the map*): Could you tell me where this is . . . ?

WAITRESS (*she checks the map*): Right out the door, one block down State Street.

PRICE: Thank you.

(*He drinks his coffee, camera follows him down the counter to the cash register.*)

HARRY: Mister, you tell me, *you* ain't from around here: how many acres does it take to support a doe all winter?

PRICE: I have no idea.

HARRY: F'*course* you don't, neither do they down state, then they should stay *out* of it. Keep the *peace,* 'stead of getting so involved with the *law.*

PRICE (*to the* WAITRESS): What do I owe you . . . ?

WAITRESS: That'll be ninety-five cents.

(*He pays her.*)

BUSINESSMAN: You want to use the *law* for something, find out who burnt the *Emporium* . . .

SECOND BUSINESSMAN: Charley Hopkins would've found him in an hour.

FARMER: You going today? The Memorial?

BUSINESSMAN: That's today, Lord, *isn't* it?

FARMER: Yep.

BUSINESSMAN: Time flies, don't it?

FARMER: I've noticed it does.

BUSINESSMAN: You going down the Memorial . . . ?

(P<small>RICE</small> *walks out of the restaurant.*)

(*ANGLE EXTERIOR: STATE STREET, TOWN OF BRADFORD. A SMALL NEW ENGLAND TOWN. He has just exited from The Coffeecorner, and behind him, in the bay window, we see the* R<small>EGULARS</small> *whose conversation we have just been hearing.* P<small>RICE</small> *stands on the sidewalk for a moment, looks up at the sky and shivers a bit. One of the* R<small>EGULARS</small> *comes out behind him, stands near him, lighting a cigarette.*)

R<small>EGULAR</small>: Just passing through?

P<small>RICE</small>: No. I think I'll stay a bit longer than that.

(*The* R<small>EGULAR</small> *moves off. Camera follows* P<small>RICE</small> *to an old station wagon at the curb. It is piled high with personal effects, clothing, and furniture.* P<small>RICE</small> *opens the passenger door, takes out a raincoat, puts it on, consults his map, and moves off down the street.*)

EXTERIOR: BRADFORD LIBRARY. DAY.

A small granite block; cut into it, a five-point star, with the name "Bradford" on it, and the badge number 2121 and "Sacred to the Memory of Charles Hopkins, Chief of Police 1968–1987."

M<small>AYOR</small> (*voice over*): What is a "good man"?

(*Angle: The* M<small>AYOR</small> *on the steps of the police department, flanked by three uniformed officers; in the foreground, twenty or so townspeople. As he speaks, it begins to rain lightly and the townspeople begin to put up umbrellas.*)

People might say, *no* man is quite as good, or quite as bad as he seems; but there *is* such a thing as a good man, and we were privileged to *know* such a man . . .

(*Angle: The group of bystanders. A* P<small>RIEST</small> *listening.*)

Charley Hopkins defined for me the meaning of Community Service, and, as I think he did for *all* of us, helped define the meaning of *Community.*

(*A young man of eighteen walks in front of the* PRIEST. *They nod to each other.*)

BILLY BATES: Morning, Father . . .

PRIEST: . . . Billy.

(BILLY *moves out of the frame.*)

MAYOR (*voice over*): Chief of Police, Past President of our Local Post of the VFW, active in *Scouting,* a grandmaster of the Masons. *Many* might say, those who did not *know* the Chief might say, "A *joiner,* a *booster,* a 'babbitt' . . ."

(*Angle: The* MAYOR.)

MAYOR: But *who* among us, does not have a Charley Hopkins story? Of the things he might have taught you . . . of a good *word* he put in for you, at *school,* to get a *job,* you never found out 'til years *later* . . . I remember one time . . .

(*Angle: The* PRIEST. PRICE *now comes into the group. It has started raining heavily.* PRICE *stands next to the* PRIEST. *We hear the* MAYOR'*s voice in the background, as* PRICE *and the* PRIEST *converse. The* PRIEST *motions for* PRICE *to come share the umbrella with him.* PRICE *demurs.*)

PRIEST: . . . Come on, don't get yourself wet.

(PRICE *moves under the umbrella with him.*)

. . . our Chief of Police. Chief Hopkins.

(PRICE *nods.*)

One year anniversary, his death.

(PRICE *nods.*)

Hell of a thing. Good man. Very good man. Died last year. Hunting accident.

PRICE: Uh-hmm.

PRIEST: A hunting accident.

PRICE: His family here?

PRIEST: Didn't have one. Someone more poetic might say the Town was his family.

PRICE: Sounds like a rare man.

PRIEST: Yes. He was.

(*Angle:* PRICE *and the ground in the foreground. The* MAYOR, *et cetera beyond.*)

MAYOR: I have in my hand *telegrams* from twenty states, from police departments, from Chiefs of Police, and from Officers that Charley met on his travels, as part of his activity in the Law Enforcement World. I will read *one* . . . (*He reads:*) "Any officer is touched when a brother gives his life in the Line of Duty. What great example, also, of a man who gave his life to a *life* of Duty. We learned from him, and we will miss him . . ."

(*The* MAYOR *concludes his speech and nods. The little groups start to break up in the rain.*)

(*Angle:* PRICE *and the* PRIEST. *Several people come up and say good-bye to the* PRIEST.)

TOWNSWOMAN (*to* PRIEST): We'll never see his like.

PRIEST: . . . Mary . . .

TOWNSWOMAN: You know, I owe him my boy's life.

PRIEST: No, I didn't know that.

TOWNSWOMAN: That time, he got into an accident, the 302. (*Beat. She moves off.*) Father . . .

(*The* PRIEST *is left alone with* PRICE.)

PRICE: Hard to replace a man like that.

PRIEST: Yes, it would be. Life goes on, though, doesn't it?

PRICE: *I've* noticed.

PRIEST: . . . problems of a Town . . . someone has got to deal with them.

PRICE: Yes.

PRIEST: Can't live in the past, now, *can* you?

PRICE: No, you can't.

PRIEST: Brings you here today?

PRICE: I . . . I came here to pay my respects. (*Pause.*) Pay my respects to the man.

(*The* PRIEST *nods. They have stopped walking.*)

PRIEST: I walk you somewhere?

PRICE: Uh, no thank you. I'm going right here.

(*They look up, they are at the Police Station.*)

PRICE: I'm the new Police Chief.

PRIEST: Figured you were.

(PRICE *starts up the steps. Camera follows him through the doors, marked "Police Department, Town of Bradford."*)

INTERIOR: BRADFORD POLICE STATION.

A woman DISPATCHER *on the radio.*

DISPATCHER: . . . that is a 201 three miles *north* of the Interstate on Highway Five. Bradford PD. Out . . . (*She turns to* PRICE:) I help you . . . ?

PRICE: Officer in charge, please.

DISPATCHER: . . . say who is calling . . . ?

(PRICE *goes in his pocket, takes out a badge, shows it to her.*)

DISPATCHER: One moment, please.

(*ANGLE INTERIOR: BEHIND THE BARRICADE. The* DISPATCHER *gets up from the desk, over her shoulder, to an assistant.*)

THE DISPATCHER: . . . mind the phones, please.

(*Camera follows her to an office marked "Chief of Police." Inside the office is* BOBBY BARNES, *thirty-five, fit, in a police uniform, talking with two deputies.*)

BARNES: . . . all kinds of static, *insurance* this, Arson *that,* we got the fellow from the State, and the *insurance* man, coming down tomorrow, 'til then let 'em gossip all they want, I think it was an accident. Now: we got a *noise* complaint, the kids, back from the Liquor Store. You lean on that man, go in there, *he* knows they're drinking, got it from the *older* boys.

DISPATCHER: Bobby . . .

BARNES: One moment: *he* knows, they're wild, they got it from his *store,* you tell him that, he'll get the message . . .

DISPATCHER (*leans in, whispers to him*): Bobby.

BARNES: Thank you. You fellows 'scuse me for a moment. (*To* DISPATCHER:) Show him in.

(*The two officers leave, as does the* DISPATCHER.)

BARNES (*into the telephone*): Helen, and tell 'em to hold all the calls this office five, ten minutes, will you . . . ?

(PRICE *comes in. The two men face each other.*)

BARNES: Afternoon . . . sit down . . . ?

(PRICE *comes over, offers his hand.*)

PRICE: John Price.

BARNES: Robert Barnes. (*Sighs.*) I've been acting Chief of Police, since Mr. Hopkins' death. (*Pause.*) Wasn't expecting you until tomorrow.

PRICE: Well, I thought I'd come in a bit early, and get *settled*, you know.

BARNES: Yes. I do. We had a, uh, we had a *memorial* today for Chief Hopkins.

PRICE: *Did* you?

BARNES: Yes. We did. We had, they had a *monument* that they unveiled . . . (*Pause.*) Testimonials . . . (*Pause.*) These *plaques* that you see, twenty-five years he served as Chief here. (*Pause.*) We've got a case now . . . building burnt on Main Street, The Emporium . . .

PRICE: Uh-huh . . . Any leads on it . . . ?

BARNES: "Leads" on it? Mister, all I got, a building burnt, we called in the *adjustors,* the State Boys, come in t'morrow, we'll see what they say, you know, it's just a *building* burnt. Eh? This is a kind of a quiet town. You see what I'm saying? Where *you* come from, I'm sure it's more *active* down there.

PRICE: That's right. I'm sure that it is.

BARNES: You'll probably miss that action.

PRICE: Part of me will, I'm sure.

BARNES: . . . aaand, we do things a little *differently* up here. You know, Chief Hopkins . . . (*pause*) . . . you see, we had a crime, we had a *situation,* something happened, he'd sit down, sit down in here, close the door, whatever it was, you see, he had the *time* for that, think: Now, who would be likely *do* a thing like that? Whatever it was, eh, from their *motives,* what he *knew* of them. He would think, then he'd call them up, and they'd come in, they'd sit in that chair, he'd *confront* them, and then they'd confess. (*Pause.*) I bet you think that's rather "folksy," *don't* you . . . ?

PRICE: I, uh, you know, I wish I lived in that sort of world. I'm glad he did. (*Pause*) I wish I had those talents.

BARNES: *Do* you . . . ?

(BILLY BATES *walks in, comes over to* BARNES.)

BILLY: Mr. Barnes . . .

BARNES: Well. It was a nice *service, wasn't* it?

BILLY: Yes sir, it was.

(OFFICER *sticks his head in the door.*)

OFFICER: Chief, we got a complaint, a prowler, again, out the new Estates.

BARNES: Gettem' out there quiet, park the car, go in on foot, and take it easy, prolly' just them kids.

(*A* SECOND OFFICER *comes in.*)

SECOND OFFICER: Chief, I talk to you a minute . . . ?

BARNES: You'll excuse me.

(BARNES *pushes past* PRICE, *who rises.* PRICE *is standing alone in the office. Looks around at the plaques on the wall.*)

(*Angle point of view: The plaques. Community Service, Boy Scouts, From a Grateful Community, Hunting Safety Instructor, et cetera.*)

DISPATCHER (*voice over*): You have a place to live in Bradford, Mr. Price . . . ?

(PRICE *turns to see the* DISPATCHER, *who has come into the office to take her coat off of the coatrack.* PRICE *turns.*)

PRICE: Pardon me.

DISPATCHER: You find a place to live? A place to live you're here?

(PRICE *takes a card out of his pocket.*)

PRICE: The Mayor, he suggested the, the Idle Hour Apartments.

DISPATCHER: Come with me, walk me out, will you . . . ?

(*Angle: The two of them walking out of the chief's office, through the small police station squad room. They walk out of the station. The* DISPATCHER *looks over her shoulder.*)

Bobby Barnes' a good man.

PRICE: Yes?

(*Camera follows them down the street. The rain is letting up, the sun is going down.*)

DISPATCHER: You a good man, Mr. Price . . .

PRICE: Well, I guess others would have to judge that.

DISPATCHER: You think of yourself as a good man?

PRICE: I try. But perhaps we aren't the best judge of ourselves.

(*They walk a while.*)

DISPATCHER: My name is May.

PRICE: John.

DISPATCHER: 'S'a long way out the Idle Hour, cold winter night.

PRICE: Is it?

DISPATCHER: Be more *comfortable,* find a place in Town. You a single man?

PRICE: Yes, I am.

(*They stop. The* DISPATCHER *gestures.*)

DISPATCHER: S'here is Anna Moore's House, lives here, her *daughter,* said that she was *thinking* maybe let a *room.* You might try here. (*Beat.*) Anybody say "Welcome to Bradford"?

PRICE: No. (*Beat.*)

DISPATCHER: Welcome to Bradford.

PRICE: Thank you.

(*The* DISPATCHER *nods, gestures at the house.* PRICE *moves up the walk, knocks on the door.*)

INTERIOR: ANNA MOORE'S HOUSE. DUSK.

A neat small Victorian House. The door is opened by a fifteen-year-old girl. PRICE *is standing at the door.*

GIRL (GINNY): May I help you?

PRICE: Um, Mrs. Moore . . .

GINNY: Mother . . . ! Mother! There's a *man* here for you . . . one moment please. Will you come in?

(*Camera follows* PRICE *into the foyer.*)

ANNA (*offstage*): Ask him to come in.

GINNY: I'm Ginny Moore.

PRICE: John Price.

(*She extends her hand. They shake hands.*)

ANNA (*offstage*): Ginny! Will you ask him to come in. I'll be . . .

GINNY: It's alright, Mother. (*To* PRICE:) Um . . . Mr. Price . . . Do we know you . . . ?

PRICE: No, if this is a bad time to . . .

(ANNA MOORE, *a very handsome woman in her late thirties, comes into the foyer, taking off an apron.*)

ANNA: Yes. Good evening.

(*The phone rings.*)

GINNY: I'll get it.

PRICE: If this is a bad time, I . . . Looks like you're making din . . .

ANNA: I'm just finishing up din . . .

PRICE: I . . .

ANNA: May I help you?

PRICE: My name is John Price. I was referred here by May . . . May . . .

ANNA: May *Fowler?* The Police Station . . . ?

PRICE: Yes. I am . . .

ANNA: You're the new Chief of Police.

PRICE: Yes.

ANNA: Welcome.

PRICE: Thank you.

ANNA: We have a fairly peaceful town. I think. We hope you like it. *We* do.

(*Pause.* GINNY *reenters.*)

GINNY: Mother: Can I go out this evening with Jimmy Clain?

ANNA: Excuse me . . . no. I'll be with you in a moment, Sweetie.

(GINNY *goes back into the other room. Pause.*)

PRICE: Um, I was told . . .

(GINNY *reenters.*)

GINNY: Excuse me, why not?

ANNA: Well, the short answer is "because," let's talk about it over dinner. Mr. . . . ?

PRICE: Price.

ANNA: You, um, what brings you here?

PRICE: Mrs. Fowler said you were considering taking in a *boarder,* and I thought . . .

ANNA: Mrs. Fowler said that?

PRICE: Yes.

ANNA: Un-huh. Well, no, no, it's something I had, I had *talked,* but I think I'd *mentioned* it at one time, but . . .

PRICE: I'm very, very sorry, please forgive me if I've inconven . . .

ANNA: No, no, not at all. It's just something. It's something, frankly, we're not quite ready to *do,* there's nothing.

PRICE: . . . No. I underst . . .

ANNA: I hope you'll *forgive* . . .

PRICE: Not at all.

(GINNY *reenters.*)

GINNY: Mother, the dinner's on.

ANNA: Yes. (*Pause.*) We'll. We look forward to . . .

GINNY: Mother. It's Mr. Price's first night in town.

(*Pause. The two women look at each other.*)

ANNA: Ah. Would you join us for dinner tonight, Mr. Pr . . . ?

PRICE: No, I really . . .

ANNA: Ginny, would you put another pl . . .

GINNY: I've already done it.

PRICE: Thank you.

(ANNA *and* GINNY *take* PRICE *into the living room, where we see three place settings in a lovely Victorian room.*)

INTERIOR: THE DINING ROOM. NIGHT.

PRICE *and* ANNA *sitting at the table.* GINNY *brings in a platter. Sits. Beat.*

ANNA: Are you a religious man, Mr. Price?

PRICE: Ma'am, I was raised as one.

ANNA: Perhaps you'd like to say Grace . . . ?

PRICE: Well, it's *been* a while . . .

ANNA: Won't you please? (*Pause.*)

PRICE: Lord, for these, thy gifts, make us truly grateful. Amen.

(*The three say "Amen."*)

ANNA: What brought you to Bradford, Mr. Price?

PRICE: Ma'am, I served twenty-five years, the City Force, I took retirement. I saw a notice, interviews, for the job of your Chief. I got the job, and here I am.

ANNA: Won't this be quite a different job from the one you're used to?

PRICE: Some ways, yes, of course, in some ways not so different.

GINNY: How is that?

PRICE: Human nature's the same, anywhere you go.

ANNA: Is that true? Yes, I suppose it is.

GINNY: What would you say, a *woman,* wouldn't let her grown daughter go out with a perfectly nice boy, *simply* because it fell afoul of an arbitrary rule that said no dating on a school night.

PRICE: Well, I'd say, first thing I learned, down the City Force: if you can *help* it, never get involved in a domestic argument.

(*The phone rings,* GINNY *goes to the phone.*)

ANNA: Tell him "no."

GINNY: I already *told* him "no," but I told him to call back in case you changed your mind.

(GINNY *leaves the room, leaving* ANNA *and* PRICE *alone.*)

ANNA: Was it a hard life down there?

PRICE: Yes. In many ways. It was a good life.

ANNA: Quite a bit of *violence,* wasn't it . . . ?

PRICE: Yes, Ma'am, yes. It was.

ANNA: . . . more *peaceful* here.

(GINNY *pops back in.*)

GINNY: *Mother,* he's going to come by, we're going to study here. (*She exits.*)

ANNA: Fine. Turn on the outside lll . . . (*Pause. To* PRICE:) What was I saying?

PRICE: You were asking if my life was violent in the City. (*Pause.*) One reason that I *came* up here (*pause*) was to *change.* (*Pause.*) To . . .

ANNA: I understand. (*Pause.*) We're all alone here, my daughter and I, Mr. Price.

PRICE: Yes Ma'am, I see that. (*Pause.*)

ANNA: Would you be keeping guns in the house?

PRICE: Yes, Ma'am, I would.

ANNA: . . . they'd be locked up . . . ?

PRICE: It's been my habit for some years.

ANNA: Ginny understands about that.

PRICE: Yes, Ma'am, I'm sure that she does.

ANNA: Then, Mr. Price, we'd be happy to have you stay here. Welcome, and we can discuss the terms tomorrow. Would that be alright?

PRICE: Yes, Ma'am, that would. Thank you.

ANNA: Not at all.

(*She stands, extends her hand. He shakes her hand.*)

Would you mind turning on the porch light, please, for Ginny's friend?

PRICE: Not at all.

ANNA: Just out the door and on your right.

(PRICE *moves to the front door.*)

(*ANGLE EXTERIOR: THE HOUSE, THE DOOR. The door opens,* PRICE *comes out on the porch. He stands alone on the porch for a moment. In the background, we see the quiet street,* PRICE, *his back to us, looking at it. He turns and looks back at the house.*)

(*Angle point of view: In the kitchen,* ANNA, *who has just come in to tell* GINNY *about the new boarder.* GINNY *seems pleased.* ANNA *picks up a platter, both go back into the dining room.*)

(*Angle:* PRICE, *looking in the window. Turns to the door, opens the door.*)

INTERIOR: POLICE STATION SQUAD ROOM. DAY.

The MAYOR *holding forth to two newsmen, several functionaries, police officers, et cetera.*

MAYOR: Mr. John Price, late Captain (*consulting his sheet*) *many* times decorated captain of the Metro Police . . . (*Gestures to sheet.*) You have his biography, the *preeminent* choice of all our applicants, and we are most, most happy to have him, and to *welcome* him, now, *Chief* of Police, Mr. John Price.

(*Applause.* PRICE *comes forward.*)

PRICE: Thank you. This is a big job. It's an important job. Much of it is within my experience, and a certain amount of it is not. I look forward to working *with* and learning *from* the Bradford Force. I'll do my best, and I thank you for your trust.

(*The meeting breaks up.* BILLY *comes by.*)

BILLY: Congratulations, Chief.

PRICE: Thank you.

(*The* PRIEST *comes by. Hands him a card.*)

PRIEST: Congratulations, Chief. Gimme' a call. Let's get together.

PRICE: Father, be assured I will.

PRIEST: We'll talk about "Social Problems." (*He scribbles on a card.*)

PRICE: Long's we can do it over a drink.

PRIEST: We'll do it tonight.

PRICE: Nothing better. I'll call you.

(*The* MAYOR *waves his good-byes. A* REPORTER *comes up to Price.*)

REPORTER: What are your plans, Chief?

PRICE: Take it easy, take it slow, learn the town, catch up on the occurrences, and ease into it.

REPORTER: Any thoughts about the arson?

PRICE: What arson?

REPORTER: The Emporium Building, yest . . .

PRICE: Well, we don't know that it's *arson,* we're going to be taking it slow . . . fellow, I've just been here five minutes . . .

SECOND REPORTER: What particularly are you going to be concentrating on?

PRICE: Crimes against the Person, Crimes against Property, Crimes against the State.

SECOND REPORTER: You think you'll be able to fill the shoes of Chief Hopkins?

PRICE: That's going to be for you to judge.

SECOND REPORTER: What will you do, specifically, to fulfill, in the Eyes of the Community . . .

PRICE: I'm going to do the job I was hired to do, to the best of my abilities. And I look forward to meeting you all personally, at some more leisurely . . . (*Starts to pull away.*)

REPORTER (*as* PRICE *starts to pull free*): You going to be working on his murder?

PRICE: I . . . uh . . . on his murder?

REPORTER: That part of your . . . ?

PRICE: It was my understanding he died in a *hunting* accident. (*Pause.*) Uh huh . . .

REPORTER: S'that high on your list?

PRICE: I'm going to jump into *all* open cases . . . you'll excuse me . . . ?

(*Camera follows him into the chief's office, where* BARNES *is talking with the officers. They all turn to look at* PRICE.)

BARNES (*trailing off*): . . . the possibilities, and *check* the alibis of . . . Good morning.

PRICE: Good morning to you all.

(*Everyone acknowledges him.*)

Right away, please, before we do anything, let's get, whoever's got the shift on Main Street, cordon off that building: let's get a rundown on the chain-of-ownership . . .

BARNES: It's a simple . . .

PRICE: . . . one moment. *While* it's fresh, and *anybody* poking in the ashes, *bring* 'em in . . .

BARNES: If, may I?

PRICE: Please.

BARNES: It's a simple fire. There's . . .

PRICE: Uh huh. Lookit, one thing I've learned, most rumors are true. Okay? Three people saying "Arson," then . . . (*Shrugs.*)

BARNES: You're making a mist . . .

PRICE: Uh-huh.

BARNES: You're making a mistake, Mister, there's a way that we *do* things up here, there's a way we *are,* don't got nothing to do with "Police" work, it's . . .

PRICE (*to the other officers*): . . . would you excuse us please . . .

(*The others look at* BARNES, *and* PRICE, *and file out.*)

PRICE: You know these people pretty well up here . . .

BARNES: Well, they're my people.

PRICE: Went to school with them, dated their sisters . . .

BARNES: All of that.

PRICE: Uh-huh . . . Been on this force long?

BARNES: Since I got back from the Navy.

PRICE: I suppose lot of the *people* hereabouts think *you* should have been made chief. (*Pause.*)

BARNES: Well, Mister, that's true.

PRICE: . . . and I know that you're one of 'em. And maybe you *should* have. Maybe you *are* the better man, but that's not the way it happened, *is* it . . . ?

BARNES: No, it's not.

PRICE: So, *I'm* gonna play out the hand I was dealt. Are *you?* (*Pause.*) It's *decision* time, the way you want it, so: you want to stay on the force, or you want to give me your badge? (*Pause.*) No *shame* in it, Officer, but you answer me.

BARNES: Alright.

PRICE: Okay, then let's see where we go.

BARNES: Alright. We'll do that.

PRICE: And I suppose you'd better start calling me "Chief."

(PRICE *goes and opens the door. Camera follows him into the next room. The group turns to look at him.*)

Now: I want the Occurrence Sheets, I want *every* open case, I don't care how far back it goes, *May:* start me with the last six months. I get through them, take me back a year, so on. I want a Community Calendar, who's meeting where, what night, the Masons, the P.T.A., who's working on this *Arson* case . . . ?

OFFICER: I am, Sir.

PRICE: My office, ten minutes, please, a full report . . . thank you, all, I've been twenty-five years the business, never saw a group of people couldn't work together, if they felt like it. (*Pause.*) I'm very proud I got this job, I mean to do my best. Anybody's got something to say, you *say* it, and I will, too. Okay . . . ? (*He goes back into his office.*) May, one moment, please . . . ?

(*Camera follows him and* MAY, *the dispatcher, into the chief's office.*)

PRICE: Oh . . . kaaay . . . get me, please, *also,* the file on Mr. Hopkins' death. That's carried as what?

MAY: Shooting accident.

PRICE: Was it?

MAY: Far as I know.

PRICE: Get me that, aaaand . . . who burnt down that building?

MAY: . . . *I* don't know.

PRICE: Who do you think? (*Pause.*) Who benefited from it?

MAY: Mrs. Amos owns the store.

PRICE: She stand to gain?

MAY: No. People up the Mall, another clothing store, the *downstate* folks. The Developers.

PRICE: That Mob Money . . . ?

MAY: I think it is . . .

PRICE: Un-huh. (*Pause.*) I'm gonna get out on the *street* today. I wanna meet you back here, four o'clock, let's go over the sheets. (*He turns back to look at the plaques.*) Get this stuff off the wall, box it and store it, please, have the wall repainted. All of that, the time I get back this afternoon, would you, please?

MAY: Yessir.

PRICE: Meeting here in three minutes.

MAY: They heard it. How do you like your coffee . . . ?

PRICE: Hot, black, straight up.

MAY: Any brand?

PRICE: Just so it don't run out.

(*She nods, goes out of the door. Beat.* PRICE *puts his briefcase up on the desk. Takes out his service revolver and holster, straps them on, takes off his jacket and hangs it over the back of his chair. Sits down. Picks up his badge off the desk.*)

(*Angle point of view insert: The badge, Bradford Chief of Police.*)

(*Angle:* PRICE *holding the badge. He puts it in his shirt pocket. Puts on eyeglasses. Takes out a file from his briefcase, goes to work on the file.*)

OFFICER (*voice over*): You ready, Chief . . . ?

(PRICE *keeps writing, does not look up.*)

PRICE: Yes, tell them to come in.

EXTERIOR: BURNT BUILDING.

The building is being cordoned off with "Police Line" tapes. PRICE *looking on. Continues down the street and into the firehouse. A fireman is polishing the engine.* PRICE *walks over to him.*

PRICE: Morning.

FIREMAN: Morning.

PRICE: John Price.

FIREMAN: Yep. I know. Jerry Bates. Glad to meet you.

PRICE: Whaddaya got on those buildings?

(FIREMAN *moves back into the ready room,* PRICE *and camera follow.*)

FIREMAN: Too early to tell, we get the report.

PRICE: What's it look like?

FIREMAN: Could go either way, way it spread. Not an *expert,* but it could go either way. The flame pattern, electrical fire, or could be arson.

PRICE: Uh-huh . . .

FIREMAN: Wouldn't want to swear to it.

PRICE: Hmm-mmm.

(*They walk around the fire engine.* PRICE *refers to a deer head on the wall.*)

You take that buck?

FIREMAN: Son, Billy. Trophy buck.

PRICE: Some animal.

FIREMAN: Yup. One shot. 30–06, two hundred yards, paced it off.

PRICE: Good shooting.

FIREMAN: . . . say it was.

(*The* FIREMAN *walks* PRICE *to the front of the firehouse and out onto the apron. There is* BILLY *about to get into his car, parked next to the firehouse.*)

PRICE: Well, I've got a few calls to make. Good meeting you, Jerry.

FIREMAN: Billy. Billy come over here.

(*The young man walks over.*)

This is Chief Price, new Chief.

PRICE: We met over the Station House.

FIREMAN: Billy's going into Law Enforcement.

PRICE: Are you?

FIREMAN: You bet he is. Starting *when* . . . ?

BILLY: . . . tomorrow.

PRICE: Really . . .

FIREMAN: Yep. Goes into the Air Force. Signed up for Air Police. Billy, Billy, uh, Billy was very close to the Chief, to Charley Hopkins . . . it was the chief that influenced him to go into the law.

BILLY: That's right.

PRICE: You going to make it a career?

BILLY: Yes, sir, I am.

PRICE: Well, you picked a good one. Could you point me toward . . . (*consults book*) the Old Town Road . . . ?

FIREMAN: You go . . . you go, uh . . . tell you the *quick* way, but you'll never *find* it. Billy!

BILLY: Yessir?

FIREMAN: You want to ride with Chief Price here, show him the Newman's Place, the Old Town Road.

BILLY: *Yessir,* glad to.

PRICE: Not necessary.

FIREMAN: It's a treat for the boy . . . you take him out there now.

PRICE: Well, thank you, I appreciate it.

(BILLY *and* PRICE *start across the street. A* TOWNSMAN *comes over to them.*)

TOWNSMAN: Heard you read out Bobby Barnes this morning.

PRICE: Word travels fast, eh?

TOWNSMAN: Mister, it's a small town.

INTERIOR: POLICE CAR. DAY.

PRICE *driving,* BILLY *riding.*

PRICE: You spent some time with the Chief?

BILLY: Quite a bit, Sir.

PRICE: Un-huh.

BILLY: He was my Hunting Safety instructor . . . and, you know, I spent a lot of time around the station house.

PRICE: Always wanted to go into the law?

BILLY: Yes, Sir, I did.

PRICE: 'One have any reason hereabouts to do him harm? (*Pause.*)

BILLY: I . . . no, sir. No one I can think of. Why do you ask?

PRICE: . . . fellow asked me a question. Stuck in my mind. What do you think about the *Arson,* Main Street?

BILLY (*thinks*): No, you mean "Who"? I . . . the book says, *Arson,* many times, the crime of a disturbed adolescent.

(PRICE *laughs.*)

PRICE: You've been doing your *homework.*

BILLY (*shrugs*): . . . other motives, of course, including revenge, and, of course, personal gain, either through collection of insurance, or elimination of a competing commercial concern.

PRICE: Son, how old are you?

BILLY: Nineteen years, sir . . .

PRICE: You want to think seriously about joining on *this* force, instead of going in the Air Police, you come by, we'll talk.

BILLY: I, well, Sir, you know.

PRICE: It's okay, just a thought. We all need allies.

(The car stops at a rural farmhouse. Camera follows the two out of the car.)

PRICE: You can come along, you want. What we got here, a complaint. Mr. Newman, it would seem, 's being accused tearing down the "No Trespassing—No Hunting" signs, his neighbor's . . . Mr. Kiernan's place. What's that mean "accused"?

BILLY: Means he was doing it.

PRICE: Why?

BILLY: Um, didn't like, folks come up, the summer folks, change the way folks live.

PRICE: Uh-huh.

BILLY: His folks been hunting on that land a long time, now man comes and posts it. *(Pause.)*

PRICE: That's the way a hunter would think.

BILLY: Yessir.

PRICE: Uh huh. Your dad showed me, that's some trophy buck you took last year. Some shooting.

(Camera follows them to the porch of the house.)

BILLY: A lucky shot.

PRICE: You going out this year?

BILLY: Already been. Didn't get nothing.

PRICE: Already been. You telling me? Season don't start until next week.

BILLY: Went out in the *bow* season.

PRICE: You went out with a bow this year?

BILLY: Yes. I, I, you know, I thought it was more *sporting*.

PRICE: Well it is *that* . . . (*Knocks on the door.*) Get anything?

(*A* MAN *answers the door. A lumberjack-looking individual around forty.*)

MAN: Yep?

PRICE: Name's John Price. I'm the new Chief of Police.

MAN: What do you want?

PRICE: Came out to get acquainted.

MAN: The summer people up the road called you in. They don't like "this" and don't like "that." I'm tearing down their signs, that's it, isn't it?

PRICE: . . . that's it, but I wouldn't worry about it.

MAN: . . . seems to me *quite* a waste of my tax money, send a man out, let alone the Chief of Police, fellow got himself a little piece of *paper* torn down off a tree.

PRICE: Couldn't agree more. (*Pause.*)

MAN: I can't say that I get you.

PRICE: Come over to *say,* that I couldn't agree more. Fellow lives here, what they live here, two, three months a year?

MAN: If that.

PRICE: A man *might* think, now, this is off the *record* here . . .

MAN: . . . I'm with you.

PRICE: . . . business do *they* have, tell someone like *you,* family's lived here, what?

MAN: Family's been on this land for two hundred years.

PRICE: . . . keep off a piece of land your *daddy* prolly hunted on . . .

MAN: . . . granddaddy, too.

PRICE: . . . land that they *surely* wouldn't *know* someone was on, as they don't get *back* there, what?

MAN: Once a year, once a year if that . . .

PRICE: They'd never know, someone was going *back* there . . .

MAN: . . . well, that is the Lord's Truth . . .

PRICE: . . . unless someone was tearing down the signs. (*Pause.*)

MAN: What did you say your name was . . . ?

(BILLY *has wandered back to the car and is holding the handset.*)

BILLY: Mr. Price . . . ?

PRICE (*to* MAN): Excuse me . . . (PRICE *goes over to the car, talks on the radio.*) Chief Price, go.

DISPATCHER (*voice over on the radio*): We have a three-car accident, the Interstate four and one half miles *north* of the Junction. Multiple fatalities. Medical and State Police responding.

PRICE: We're on our way. (*He gets into the car. To* BILLY:) Buckle it up tight.

EXTERIOR: ROADSIDE. INTERSTATE. DAY.

A car wreck, paramedics, police cruisers. PRICE's *car pulls up.* PRICE *gets out, followed by* BILLY. *Walks over to a* TROOPER. *As he walks over, he puts his shield on his jacket pocket.*

PRICE: Whadda we got?

TROOPER: Three car. First guy jumps the divider, headon the second car, three dead, mother, two young girls. Third car tries to swerve, over the embankment, and they're down there . . .

(*Camera follows* PRICE, *the* TROOPER, *and* BILLY *to the side of the road. Down below is a totaled car, and paramedics coming up the hill. One shakes his head.*)

(*The group starts back toward one of the cars on the side of the road. One man is being taken out on a stretcher. In the background, another Bradford police cruiser pulls up. Another* TROOPER *comes up to the group.*)

SECOND TROOPER: You got a car reeking of liquor and a broken bottle in there.

(*He hands the wallet to the* FIRST TROOPER, *who hands it to* PRICE. PRICE *calls* BILLY *over, shows him the wallet.*)

PRICE: This mean anything to you?

BILLY: Yes, Sir, I knew him.

(BARNES *comes out of the cruiser, over to* PRICE *and the group.*)

BARNES: What is it?

(PRICE *hands him the wallet,* BARNES *looks at it.*)

BARNES: Is he dead?

PRICE: If he ain't, I think he's going to wish he was. You want to meet me at the hospital . . . ?

(*They nod to the* TROOPER.)

TROOPER: Chief, wish we coulda' met under better circumstances . . .

(PRICE *nods. Looks back at the scene.*)

INTERIOR: HOSPITAL WAITING ROOM. NIGHT.

PRICE, BILLY. *In the background,* BARNES *talking to a doctor, an officer at his side.*

BARNES: . . . need a blood sample, alcohol content, get it *right* now, Officer, you stick with it, watch 'em *draw* it, *seal* it, and you sign the seal. Draw *two,* you sign 'em both. You hear me . . . ?

(PRICE *turns.*)

(*Angle: The* PRIEST, *coming into the hospital.* PRICE *goes over to him, hands him a list.*)

PRIEST: All dead?

PRICE: . . . all but the man.

PRIEST: Uh-huh . . .

PRICE: . . . he has a drinking problem, did he . . . ? (*Beat.*)

PRIEST: Did he?

PRICE: Looks like it. We'll find out tomorrow, we get the tests. (*To* BARNES:) The chain of evidence tend to get muddy sometimes?

BARNES: The man is well liked in these parts . . .

PRICE (*nods*): Yeah. That's a tough one.

(*The* PRIEST *comes up.*)

PRIEST: Seems we'll be postponing our drink this evening.

(*A* NURSE *calls them.*)

NURSE: Father . . .

(*They turn to look at a man who has just come into the hospital waiting room.*)

PRIEST (*sotto*): His wife and daughters.

(PRICE *takes a deep breath. Starts over to the man.*)

PRIEST (*stopping him*): No, he's one of mine. I'll tell him.

PRICE (*to* BILLY): Can you get home from here?

BILLY: Yessir. Is there anything I can do?

PRICE: No. (*He checks his list.*) I've got to take some people some bad news.

EXTERIOR: BRADFORD MAIN STREET. NIGHT.

PRICE *walks down the quiet street. An* OFFICER *falls into step beside him.*

OFFICER: A long day, sir.

PRICE: Yes.

OFFICER: Thrown right into it.

PRICE: Well, it never stops, does it.

OFFICER: No, sir, it does not. (*Pause.*) *Changes* a little, time-to-time, though . . .

PRICE: . . . that's right.

OFFICER: Summer people falling out the boat; winter people falling through the ice.

PRICE: Uh-huh. You keep an eye, your rounds—the burnt-out building.

OFFICER: Yes, sir, I will.

PRICE: Good night.

(PRICE *has arrived at* MRS. MOORE's *house. He starts up the walkway, turns off the light, tries the door. It is open, he enters.*)

INTERIOR: MOORES' HOUSE. NIGHT.

PRICE *enters, hangs up his coat. Sees something. Looks.*

Angle point of view: MRS. MOORE, *in a wrapper, coming out of the kitchen.*

PRICE: Um, evening.

ANNA: Good evening.

PRICE: Uh, you, you weren't waiting up for me?

ANNA: No, not at all. Ginny's out on a date . . . I'm up late most nights, reading. Anyway. (*Pause.*) Made a pot of tea. Would you like some?

PRICE: That would be very nice. Thank you.

ANNA: How was your first day?

PRICE: Excuse me?

ANNA: How was your first day?

PRICE: Well, they had me earning my money.

ANNA: It was a hard day?

PRICE: Yes, parts of it.

(*She comes in with the tea.*)

Thank you.

ANNA: Can you get some rest now?

PRICE: Yes. I have a little work to do, *I'll* wait up for your daughter, if you like.

ANNA: That's alright.

PRICE: How is she?

ANNA (*pause*): She's seeing the wrong boy . . .

PRICE (*smiles*): Well, a lot of us who *were* that wrong boy, I know, we were fairly *grateful* . . . I don't suppose that's any comfort.

ANNA: No. But thank you for the effort. (ANNA *gets up.*)

PRICE: Your door was open?

ANNA: I'm sorry . . . ?

PRICE: Your front door.

ANNA: Yes.

PRICE: You should probably keep it locked.

ANNA: You know, the town is fairly safe . . .

PRICE: Yes, you . . . you have a *policeman* living here, now, is all that I thought, and sometimes . . .

ANNA: Ah. I never thought of that.

PRICE: And sometimes . . .

ANNA: No. No. (*Pause.*) It's not that kind of town. And even if it is, I'm going to live as if it's not. But thank you for thinking of us. Good night. You have a good rest.

PRICE: Good night. See you tomorrow.

(*He spreads out papers on the dining room table and starts to work.*)

INTERIOR: BRADFORD POLICE STATION. DAY.

Chief's office. PRICE *just coming in.* MAY *is bringing him coffee. Puts a list in front of him.*

MAY: State Fire Inspector's out on the site, the Emporium . . .

PRICE: . . . good.

MAY: Got a report, the Developers, the Mall, heard you were *interested, their* interest, as competitors, the Clothing Store.

PRICE: *Did* they . . .

MAY: They'd like to meet with you, their offices, at one.

PRICE: "Their" offices . . . *they're* dreaming. Tell them I can spare 'em five minutes, *here* one o'clock, let's see if they're guilty.

MAY: Right. Tomorrow, twelve noon, you are invited. Lunch, the Rotary, the Country House. They're *very* nice guys . . .

PRICE: How's the food?

MAY: . . . the food is good, too . . .

PRICE: Alright.

MAY: Here is the file you requested.

PRICE: Which file is that?

MAY: The shooting of Chief Hopkins.

(*He takes the file.*)

PRICE: They never found the guy . . .

MAY: What guy? Stray shot, some hunter . . .

(PRICE *looks at the file.*)

And yesterday's Occurrence Sheets. Here are purchase orders . . . last month's cash flow, a request from the High School, you come to address the . . .

PRICE: Yeah, yeah, yeah, waaiii . . . can I . . . I'd like to meet with . . . they have a psychologist the High School?

MAY: They have a guidance counselor.

PRICE: I'd like to meet with him . . .

MAY: . . . it's a her.

PRICE: Earliest. If they could come in . . .

MAY: Alright, and *this* is called "coffee."

PRICE: Send him in.

(MAY *goes to the door, motions* BARNES *in.*)

PRICE: Listen, you're doin' a real good job, the hospital last night.

BARNES: . . . uh, thank you . . .

PRICE: I know, you do it for a living, you don't need any praise, *you* were the Chief, you'd be doing the same thing, the men under *you,* so gimme' a break. Our prominent attorney at the hospital . . . ?

BARNES: He's still hanging on.

PRICE: What's the prognosis?

BARNES: He'll live, he ain't gonna walk again.

PRICE: The blood alcohol?

BARNES: Drunk as a Lord.

PRICE: Well, *that'sa* surprise.

(*The phone rings.*)

PHONE (*voice over*): Chief. Bill Simons on his way up.

PRICE: Who is this?

BARNES: Bill Simons, big car dealership, the 201. And President the Masons Lodge . . . a friend of Mr. Ellman, who killed those fine folks with his car last night.

PRICE: I see.

(*There is a knock at the door.*)

Thank you, Bob.

BARNES: You don't mind, I think I should stay.

PRICE: Alright.

(*Opens the door.* BILL SIMONS *comes in.*)

SIMONS: Chief, Bill Simons . . .

PRICE: Glad to meet you, Sir. Sit down.

SIMONS: Uh, Mr. Price: (*Pause.*) Richard Ellman . . . Uh huh . . . Uh huh . . . You know, this is a good town, here, Mr. Price.

PRICE: Yes, I know that it is.

SIMONS: And there's a lot of good people in this town, and Dick Ellman is one of them.

PRICE: He killed four people last night, Sir.

SIMONS: I . . .

PRICE: He didn't mean to do it, but he might as *well* have.

SIMONS: You prosecute that man for murder, Mr. Price, you're making a mistake.

PRICE: What he gets *prosecuted* for's not my department, Sir, but that is the *charge* that I'll serve on him.

SIMONS: You're making a mistake.

PRICE: That may well be. (*Pause.*)

SIMONS: Alright. (*Pause.*) You know, I *voted* for you, for this job.

PRICE: I'll try to earn your trust.

(SIMONS *leaves the office.* BARNES *and* PRICE *look at each other. Beat. There is a knock on the door. The* MAYOR *enters.*)

PRICE: Thank you, Bob.

(BARNES *nods, leaves the office.*)

MAYOR: Chief?

PRICE: Sir, it ain't pretty.

MAYOR: It's . . . um . . .

(PRICE *reads from the form.*)

PRICE: Mr. Richard Ellman. D.W.I. Alcohol content of *.10%* driving while under suspension, two priors, D.W.I. And if I can be frank, Sir, I understand he was a, I beg your pardon, is a prominent citizen, and an attorney, we'll assume there were a couple more he walked away from. The guy is an alcoholic, he should never have been driving a car, the Courts *said* so, and he's driving anyway. That's too bad in the first place, he goes out and kills four people. (*Pause.*) And the law says: vehicular homicide, it's manslaughter.

(*The* MAYOR *nods, leaves.* PRICE *is left alone at his desk, looking through the file on the murder of Chief Hopkins.*)

"Chief Hopkins" attendance, law enforcement seminar, San Juan, Puerto Rico, January . . . Reno, Nevada . . .

(MAY *comes in.*)

The Chief had a lot of *time* on his hands, *didn't* he . . . ?

MAY: Waaall, he liked to travel in his off-time.

PRICE: God bless him, is it always so busy around here?

MAY: You having second thoughts?

PRICE: I thought the country was s'posed to be peaceful . . .

MAY: You can't prove it by me. Ellen Rice, Guidance Counselor, Central High School, would be glad to come in this afternoon after school. What's that about, if I may ask?

PRICE: "Arson," I have been reminded, is often a crime of a disturbed adolescent, seeking adult recognition.

MAY: Oh . . .

INTERIOR: LIBRARY. DAY.

PRICE *in the stacks. Taking a book out. Camera follows him back to his table where there are several books on psychology.* PRICE *sits, reads.*

PRIEST (*voice over*): How you doing, John?

PRICE: Fine, Father, yourself?

PRIEST: I'm alright.

PRICE: Nice library you've got here.

PRIEST: We like it.

PRICE: Spent a lot of time in libraries . . .

PRIEST: *Did* you . . . ?

(PRICE *picks up books, returns them to the main counter, says "Thank You." He and the* PRIEST *walk out.*)

PRICE: I was a beat cop. Roof over your head, warm *radiators* . . . nothing like a library.

(*Angle exterior: The library.*)

PRIEST: Where are you off to?

PRICE: Meeting with some real-estate types.

PRIEST: I'll walk with you.

(*The* PRIEST *and* PRICE *start to stroll down the street.*)

Hard night, last night.

PRICE: Yes, I suppose it was. Seems, though, that that's what they *pay* you for.

PRIEST: You ever need to talk about it, call me up.

PRICE: Seems to me we had a date last night, to get together.

PRIEST: Yes, we did.

PRICE: . . . before it heated up. Waaall, one thing you can say for it, the *work's* steady. You know. I wanted to ask you 'bout Chief Hopkins.

PRIEST: . . . yes . . . ?

PRICE: I've been doing some *research*. A, uh, a *reporter* asked me a *question* . . .

(*They have arrived at the bus station.* BILLY BATES *comes over to them.*)

BILLY: Father!

PRIEST: Hello, Billy. Today, ah, today . . .

(BILLY'S *father comes over.*)

FIREMAN: That's right. Off to the Wars.

PRIEST: Well, all the best.

PRICE: All the best. (*To the* BUS STATION ATTENDANT:) Waiting for the One O'clock bus . . . ?

ATTENDANT: . . . going to be ten minutes late.

(BILLY *takes* PRICE *aside.*)

BILLY: I wanted to thank you.

PRICE: To thank me for what?

BILLY: For taking me along last night.

PRICE: Well, you did good. You kept your mouth shut and your eyes open . . . and *listen* to me, you *go* off to the Air Force, you see the world, learn what they got to teach you, you come *back,* I'm still *here,* you want a job, come in my office and we'll have a talk.

BILLY: Thank you.

(PRICE *refers to* BILLY's *luggage.*)

PRICE: You're traveling light?

BILLY: Well . . . it's a new life . . .

PRICE: That's right. You're not taking your guns with you? They let you take 'em in the Air Force . . . ?

BILLY: I just had the one, the deer rifle, 'n'I traded it off, buy my bow.

(PRICE *nods.* JERRY *calls* BILLY *over to say good-bye to some people. A police cruiser with* BARNES *pulls up.*)

BARNES: . . . I've got some information for you . . .

PRICE: Can't get away from the office, eh?

BARNES: Yes, look . . .

PRICE: . . . uhhhh . . . The *old* Chief, eh, how'd he manage it, got so much time off, running here, running there . . . (*Pause.*)

BARNES: I don't know.

PRICE: Running off, this *convention,* that *seminar* . . . (*Pause.*) How did he manage that?

BARNES: Well: he'd been in the job a long time, he . . .

PRICE: . . . uh-huh . . .

BARNES: . . . he *designed* it that way. He needed time away, keep *current* with the current law enforcement . . .

(*Over the P.A. we hear "The one o'clock bus south has left Lynn Junction, and is due to arrive this terminal approximately five minutes."*)

Why are you asking me this?

PRICE: Because I *telephoned* several of those organizations, the Chief was supposed to've gone to, those conventions. And you know, he never went. (*Pause.*) He never went to any of 'em. (*Pause.*)

BARNES: I know that.

PRICE: You do. How come?

BARNES: I checked 'em out, too.

PRICE: *Did* you . . .

BARNES: Yes.

PRICE: He was there, in the cities, according to the airline tickets, vouchers, so on, but he never made it to the Seminars. (*Pause.*) Mister Barnes. (*Pause.*) What do you think he was *doing* there? (*Pause.*) Is there something I should know? Down there, doing something he couldn't do here? (*Pause.*)

BARNES: You don't . . . you don't like to live a life founded on rumors . . .

(PRICE *turns to look at* BILLY BATES.)

PRICE: The *kid* spent a lot of time at the Station House.

BARNES: . . . why do you bring him up?

PRICE: Because I never heard of any kid would trade away a *rifle* he took a trophy buck with. (*Pause.*) Did *you* . . . ? (PRICE *turns to the* BUS ATTENDANT, *gestures back at a storeroom.*) Can I use this room, please . . . ?

ATTENDANT: Yessir.

(PRICE *walks over to the group of* JERRY, BILLY, *the* PRIEST, *et cetera.*)

PRICE: Can I steal Billy away for a second . . . ?

(*He walks* BILLY *back into the storeroom.*)

BILLY: What is it, Chief . . . ?

(*Pause.*)

PRICE: When'd you decide you were going to go into the Air Force, Bill?

BILLY: 'Bout, 'bout a *year* ago, I . . .

PRICE: After Chief Hopkins died.

BILLY: Yes.

PRICE: His death disturbed you.

(*Pause.*)

BILLY: Yes.

PRICE: You wanted to get out of town?

BILLY: Yes. My, my, my father, I wanted to, if I was going to go into the Police, to go right away, but my father said to finish High School, so I . . . (*pause*) so I . . . (*pause*) I . . . (*Pause.*) You know, when you want to *do* thing, when something *happens,* you know what I mean, when, when . . . (*Pause.*)

PRICE: Where's the deer rifle, Billy? (*Pause.*)

BILLY: What rifle?

PRICE: What did you do, *bury* it? (*Pause.*) You buried it, is that it? Uh-huh, *you* don't have to tell me where it is. (*Pause.*) You were *hunting* with him? Is that the thing? He took you *hunting?* (*Pause.*) What did he *do* to you? (*Pause.*) Hmmm . . .

BILLY: . . . I . . .

PRICE: D'you *mean* to shoot him? (*Pause.*) Well, I suppose it comes down to the same thing. *Doesn't it?* (*Pause.*)

BILLY: I . . . Oh God. I don't know what to do. I . . . I . . . (*Pause.*) I . . . It was . . . I didn't *mean* to . . .

(*Announcement over the P.A.: "The one o'clock bus from Lynn Junction is now arriving, passengers for Weston, Hereford, Blake, and Johnson. Your one o'clock bus arriving at the terminal."*)

What am I going to *do;* what am, what will *happen* to my *family?* I . . . I didn't *mean* it! I didn't *mean* it . . . no one can *help* me . . . no one can *help* me . . . what am I going to *do* . . . ? Help me . . . (*pause*) . . . Help me.

(*The door opens, they look up to see the* PRIEST. *Pause.*)

BILLY: Father . . . *help* me . . .

PRIEST: The, uh, the *bus* is here. (*Pause.*) I came in to say the bus is here. Mr. Price . . . ?

(*He leaves. Beat.*)

PRICE: Uh-huh. Alright. What happened, that's something that happened. It's done. It's not your secret, see, I know it, too, 'cause you confessed to me. And you know what I told you? *Live* with it. You told your story and the law don't want you. Far as I'm concerned. This never took place, you and me, you ask me, I deny it. Far as you, what happened, you told me it was a hunting accident, and I believe it. Suck it up and live with it. It happened a long time ago, and no one's going to be served by bringing it up. He said the bus is here.

(PRICE *walks to the door, he opens the door.*)

(*ANGLE EXTERIOR: THE BUS LOADING.* PRICE *coming out, followed by* BILLY.)

FIREMAN: What, you getting some advice the Chief, here, Bill?

(BILLY *nods.*)

PRICE: So long, now . . .

(BILLY *gets on the bus.*)

PRIEST: What was that about?

PRICE: Saying good-bye. (PRICE *walks over to* BARNES.) You said you have some information for me.

BARNES: Fire Investigator, the State, says it's an electrical fire, pure and simple. No question.

PRICE: Uh-huh. Well, I guess that I was wrong.

BARNES (*gestures*): I . . . anything you want to tell me?

PRICE: Nope.

BARNES: You sure?

PRICE: Nothing to tell. Isn't that the way, sometimes, you get het up, it all comes down to nothing. Just like you said.

(The bus is pulling out. The PRIEST *calls over to* PRICE.*)*

PRIEST: . . . you stop down by the Rectory tonight.

PRICE: *Yessir.*

*(*PRICE *walks* BARNES *over to the squad car.)*

PRICE: I had a meeting with those real-estate folks; we can cancel it.

BARNES: Alright. You want a ride back, Chief?

PRICE: Think I'm going to walk.

(The squad car pulls out, PRICE *starts down the street. He walks past* MRS. MOORE, *who is coming out of a grocery store with a couple of bags.)*

ANNA: Ah. Supper tonight. Seven o'clock. Will your work keep you, do you think, or will you be home?

PRICE: No, Ma'am. Seven o'clock. I'll be there.

(She smiles, moves off. He walks down the street by himself. A PASSERBY *nods at him.)*

PASSERBY: Chief . . .

*(*PRICE *nods in return.)*

The Museum of Science and Industry Story

"Science and Industry Alter
and Illuminate our Time."
—JOHN LEE BEATTY

Dramatis Personae

MUSEUM GUIDE
ALBERT LITKO
RUDY
PIERRE
JOHN
CLORIS
TIMMY O'SHEA
HARRY
STOSH ZABISCO
BO LUND
LARS SVENSON
DIETER GROSS
POLICEMAN
SECOND POLICEMAN
POTAWATAMIES
FARMERS
MINERS

A helicopter shot of the Museum of Science and Industry.

MUSEUM GUIDE (*voice over*): . . . between the South Side community of Hyde Park, and Lake Michigan; a Recreation, an Educational experience, a Monument to Humankind's struggle to Rise from the Muck and Goo, and get the upperhand over its environment . . .

(*A shot of the foyer of the museum, by the main doors. The* MUSEUM GUIDE *is seen ushering out a group of Japanese businessmen, to whom he has been giving his lecture. [Their translator can be heard mumbling softly behind the lecture.]* ALBERT LITKO, *a good-looking fellow in his twenties, is seen on the upper level of the foyer, staring at the main doors.*)

. . . Chicago's famed Museum of Science and Industry . . .

(*The* MUSEUM GUIDE *continues to usher his charges out the main doors, along with other groups and individuals, who file out toward the parking lot. It is obviously closing time. An* OLD WOMAN *leaving the museum steps on* ALBERT'S *foot.*)

OLD WOMAN: I stepped on your foot.

ALBERT: Mmmmm.

(*The* OLD WOMAN *continues on her way.*)

GUIDE: . . . home of the famous Two-Speed Clock; The Living Cantaloupe; . . . The U-505 Submarine (the First Foreign Man of War captured on the High Seas in a Coon's Age) . . .

(*The* GUIDE *continues as voice over,* ALBERT *is seen to leave his vantage point and move to the public telephones.*)

. . . Planes, Trains, all sorts of Weird Objects, various Exhibits, a Huge model Railroad, and stuff too numerous to mention; open most of the time to one and all, and now bidding you, each and every one, from the citizens of Chicago, to the denizens of famed Nippon, a fond "Sayonara."

(ALBERT *is now seated at a phone, has dialed, and listens to ringing.*)

ALBERT: Hello?

Where *are* you?

Albert.

Albert *Litko.*

(*As* ALBERT *talks we see the lights, section by section, being extinguished in the museum.*)

At the Museum.

Waiting for *you.*

Well, we *did.*

We certainly *did.*

Well, *I* thought we did.

I'm sorry, too.

At the Museum, I told you.

It's okay. What are you doing *tonight?*

Oh. (*Long pause.*)

(*The camera tracks through the upper level of the museum, shooting down at the main floor, revealing total absence of humanity, and darkness.*)

What are you doing *tomorrow* night?

Oh.

No. I'm not. I'm not.

No. Don't be silly.

No. Okay.

I . . . uh . . . look, good-bye, okay?

(*The camera returns to* ALBERT *seated at the telephone.*)

I swear I'm not hurt. On my mother's deathbed. I swear.

Okay. I will.

Okay.

Okay, good-bye.

(*The phone is obviously hung up on the other end. We hear a disconnect signal coming from the phone, which* ALBERT *still holds in his hand. A pause, then* ALBERT *utters an inchoate cry and whacks the telephone with the handset. We hear a slight "ding."* ALBERT *checks the coin return and finds out that it's his dime.*)

Ha ha ha ha ha.

(*He hangs up the phone. He gets up and starts to walk, in a controlled and dignified manner, to the doors. The camera follows behind him. He arrives at the closed doors, tries the handle. It is locked. He tries another door, he tries the last door. He finds that he is, in fact, locked in. He screams and starts pounding on the door.*)

Vixen! Siren! I give my *heart* to you, I give my *soul* to you, I get locked *in,* it's *dark* (Oh, God, I'm *such* a sucker for a kind word) . . . I'm *scared, it does not pay to get involved.* I don't *care,* I'm going on *record,* I've said it, and I'm glad.

(*He stops pounding and composes himself. He adjusts his clothing and starts trying to find a way out of the museum. The camera follows him walking through the main hall. As he walks he mumbles.*)

. . . safety precautions . . .

. . . inadequate *crowd* control . . .

. . . social consciousness . . .

. . . *savoir faire* . . .

. . . 'preciate me someday when I'm dead . . .

(*Over his mumbling we hear a voice singing "K. C. Moan." *ALBERT* stops and tries to identify the direction from whence the voice comes. Having identified it, he proceeds toward it. The camera follows him into the hall containing the Santa Fe model railroad. The song has now changed to "The Atcheson Topeka, and the Santa Fe." *ALBERT* follows the song around to the east end of the exhibit, and finds an old black man seated at the controls, singing. This is *RUDY*. He is dressed in traditional railroad work attire which is incredibly worn and old. He is working the controls. *RUDY* stops singing and begins shouting at the trains.*)

RUDY: 'Kay, less gettem rollin', ain't got all night. Lettem go, three cars. Three cars.

ALBERT: 'Scuse me.

RUDY: Yup?

ALBERT: I'm locked in.

RUDY: Gest you was. (*To exhibit:*) Come on, *hump* those cars.

ALBERT: Uh . . . uh, what are you doing?

RUDY: *Look* like I'm doin'? (*To exhibit:*) *Now* you talkin'. You talkin' now. Keep rollin'. (*To* ALBERT:) I'm switchin'.

ALBERT: Oh.

RUDY (*to exhibit*): Two more, two more, lettem go. (*To* ALBERT:) Stan' back there, willya, son?

ALBERT: I'm locked in here.

RUDY: I see that. (*Hands him plug tobacco.*) Have a chaw, feel better.

ALBERT: No thank you, I don't chew.

RUDY: Bes' thing in the worl', you *loss*, sit down, have a chaw, think things over.

ALBERT: I'm not lost. I'm locked in.

RUDY: 'Mounts to the same thing. You jes' here for the night, then.

ALBERT: What do you mean?

RUDY: All I mean, you jes' here for the *night*. (*To exhibit:*) Whoa! *Slow* it down, there. Ho up. Ho up. Take a break. (*To* ALBERT:) We goan take a little break here. Chaw?

ALBERT: Uh, no thank you.

RUDY: Yes *sir. Hell* of a good deal workin' indoors. Course, the *trains* are smaller . . .

ALBERT: Uh huh . . .

RUDY: But that's jes' common *sense*. You gonna work indoors, you got reglar size rollin' stock, you got to get y'self a buildin' size of I don't know *what*. Huh?

(ALBERT *nods his head.*)

Ain't so bad in here. No. You only stayin' the night, huh?

ALBERT: I got locked in.

RUDY: I been here mos' eleven years. Nigh on twelve years. Yup.

(RUDY *leaves the control board and wanders to the real locomotive located about twenty feet from same. He seats himself at the controls,* ALBERT *follows him.*)

Close on twelve years. (*Pause.*) Pensioned off in Sixty, Ruth died Sixty . . . uh . . . Sixty-Two . . . wandered in here one day . . . Nineteen and Sixty-Three. I think I'm going to sing here.

(RUDY *sings "Rudy's Song." A song of his fascination with trains since boyhood . . . of his wish to be an engineer . . . of his youth working in*

Pullman cars . . . of his working as a fireman . . . of his wife, their
marriage, their children . . . of his compulsory retirement, the death of his
wife, and his old age. He finishes his song.)

Yup.

ALBERT: And so now you work for the Museum now? You work for the
Museum Railroad?

RUDY: I'm not an idiot, son. I'm *old*, but I got my senses intack. The
Museum don't got a *railroad*, what the Museum got, the Museum got
a *model* railroad.

ALBERT: Yes.

RUDY: Well, it's apparent. An' I doan work *for* them . . .

ALBERT: No?

RUDY: No, I jes' kind of . . . *work* here. I mean, what for they goan
pay someone good cash come in here switch all the *rollin'* stock at
night? It's a useless expenditure their part. Huh?

ALBERT: I suppose so.

RUDY: No supposin' in it. It's outright featherbedding. (An' I have
been a Union Man all my life, y'unnerstand, but some things I do not
hold with.)

ALBERT: Uh-huh.

RUDY: What I mean, a man has got to have his *pride* (This is common
knowledge). You stick him on a job he doan *do* nothin' . . . I mean,
you stick him on a job he doan *do* nothin' all day long, all day long he
got nothin' to *do*. (You see what I'm sayin'?)

ALBERT: Yes.

RUDY: An' in the same spirit, you take a man, prime of his life, not a goddamned thing in the *worl'* the matter with him, an' you tell him to punch out, go home, doan come back . . . well, I doan got to *tell* you what *this* is. (*Pause.*) So, in answer to your question, no, I do not work for the Museum, as any fool can plainly see.

ALBERT: Oh.

(*Pause.*)

RUDY: I free-lance.

ALBERT: Can you help me get outta here?

RUDY: What?

ALBERT: I want to go home.

RUDY: Doan you *go* home, then?

ALBERT: The Museum is locked.

RUDY: Doan you *relax,* then? (See what I'm sayin'?) Come on, I'm goan take a break anyway. See if we can't get you out of here.

(*They leave the Santa Fe exhibit, and walk toward the Harvester Farm.*)

You ever live in the country?

ALBERT: No. We lived in the *suburbs* a little.

RUDY: Ain't the same thing.

(*A huge war cry is heard, and a boomerang narrowly misses* RUDY'S *head*.)

(*Loudly*): Sonsabitches.

PIERRE (*voice over*): Get you next time.

RUDY: Hell you say. (*He picks up boomerang. To* ALBERT:) Sonabitch can't even get the goddam thing come *back.*

(*They walk on.*)

Born an' *raised* in the country. Yup. Doan tell *me* 'bout country life. Uh-*uh. Hate* it in the country. Got out firs' chance I got.

(*They approach the farm.*)

Smoke, noise, *action*, some kine *movement* . . . you see what I'm gettin' at?

ALBERT: Yes.

RUDY: You hungry?

ALBERT: I . . . uh . . . a little. I'm a bit confused.

RUDY: You wan' a chaw?

ALBERT: No thank you.

(*They come upon a pastoral scene at the farm [appropriately enough]. Six or eight aged hippies dressed in denim overalls and grown a bit paunchy [perhaps led by Bruce Vilanch] are seated at a table covered with dishes full of candy bars, Twinkies, etc., and pitchers of Pepsi.* JOHN, *the leader of the farmers, approaches* RUDY *and* ALBERT.)

JOHN: Rudy.

RUDY: Evenin', John.

JOHN: Who's your friend?

RUDY: *Frien'* of mine.

ALBERT: Albert Litko, I got locked in.

JOHN: Glad to meet you.

ALBERT: Likewise.

JOHN: Sit down, sit down.

(ALBERT *sits down*.)

Make yourself at home, any friend of Rudy's is always welcome.

RUDY: Glad to hear you say that, John.

JOHN: Wouldn't say it if I didn't mean it.

RUDY: That so?

JOHN: Yes. (*To* ALBERT:) Dig in, dig in. Bet you aren't used to country food, eh?

ALBERT: No.

JOHN: No two ways about it. No substitute for it. Eh, Rudy?

RUDY: *Hate* the country.

JOHN: Cloris! Cloris, bring these boys some milk. (*To* ALBERT:) Never too old for milk.

(CLORIS, *an attractive woman in her early thirties, decked out in hippie farm fashion, appears with a pitcher full of Pepsi.* CLORIS *pours a glass of Pepsi for* ALBERT.)

ALBERT: This is not milk.

JOHN: I know that.

ALBERT: This is Pepsi.

JOHN: Of course it's Pepsi. If you only use the common sense God gave you you will see that yonder cows are about as fradulent as they could ever *be*. They're made of *wood*. They cannot *give* milk. We *know* this.

RUDY: Can't *get* milk from a cow like that.

ALBERT: I see that.

RUDY: Only thing you get is disappointed.

ALBERT: I can see that.

JOHN (*to* ALBERT): Would you please pass the milk pitcher. (ALBERT *does so; to assembled* FARMERS:) Friends, I think it would not be inappropriate at this point to offer a small display of gratitude for this meal which we enjoy.

(*The* FARMERS *stop and sing "The Farmers Song." The song of how good it is to get back to the land and discover one's roots and embrace nature. When they finish their song,* ALBERT *pulls* RUDY *aside and interrogates him.*)

ALBERT: Who are these people?

RUDY: Farmers. Live in the Farm.

ALBERT: Uh, where do they come from?

RUDY: Mosly they folk wander over from the University Chicago, side to stay.

ALBERT: What are they *doing* here?

RUDY: They farmin'. That one he puts bunches of knots in string, and they got a girl signed to make up poems 'bout the reaper. They real into handicraft.

(JOHN *rises and sings "The Song of the Arid Intellectual Life." The following dialogue takes place in back of his first chorus:*)

ALBERT: But they can't live off *farming.*

RUDY: They live off th' vending machines downstairs.

ALBERT: Oh.

RUDY: See, you got John a little mad, talkin' bout the milk. Milk machine's buss, so they got to drink Pepsi.

ALBERT: Oh.

(JOHN *finishes "The Song of the Arid Intellectual Life," and sits down to the approbation of his comrades.*)

RUDY: Real well sung, John.

JOHN: I'm glad you think so. (*To* ALBERT:) So, what do *you* do?

ALBERT: I'm locked in.

JOHN (*as to some novelty*): Oh!

ALBERT: Could you help me get out?

JOHN: It would be my pleasure to.

RUDY: Please pass the Twinkies.

ALBERT: Thank you.

JOHN: Not at all. Cloris!

(CLORIS *appears.*)

CLORIS: John?

JOHN: This is . . .

ALBERT: Albert Litko.

(CLORIS *nods.*)

JOHN: Albert has been locked in . . .

CLORIS: Uh huh . . .

JOHN: And would like to be shown the way out.

CLORIS: Glad to do it.

JOHN (*rising*): You're in good hands.

ALBERT: I'm sure. I, uh, well . . . (*He rises and moves to* CLORIS. *To* RUDY:) Well, It's been a pleasure meeting you.

RUDY (*rising from his plate*): Likewise.

(CLORIS *begins to lead* ALBERT *out of the museum. As they move away from the table and into the darkened museum we hear the eating noises of the* FARMERS *in the background:* "Anybody want a Snickers?" *etc.*)

ALBERT: Someone threw a boomerang at us earlier.

CLORIS: Goddamn Potawatamies.

ALBERT: Oh. Does, uh, does anybody know you people are in here?

CLORIS: Well, of course.

ALBERT: Oh.

CLORIS: We are not loafers, we are not moochers. We are not here at the whim of some demented officialdom. We perform a useful agrarian function.

ALBERT: Yes?

CLORIS: Yes. Many things. We, uh . . . we polish the *cows* . . . *Many things* . . .

(*As they walk past the entrance to the coal mine they hear singing. They see a group of old men [some in wheelchairs] clustered around the entrance, and before them, on a soapbox, is* TIMMY, *a seventy-year-old man dressed in the style of the thirties. He has on baggy pants, suspenders, a shirt with the collar detached, and a battered felt hat on the back of his head. He is trying to lead the men before him in a rendition of "Miner's Life."*)

ALBERT: What's that?

CLORIS: Miners' meeting.

ALBERT: Could we watch for a minute?

CLORIS: You're the guest.

(*They stop and listen. The song is finished, and* TIMMY *starts to speak.*)

TIMMY: World's full of freeloaders, friends: "Lemme see what the Union's going to do for me." Full of fellas kind enough bet on a sure thing came in yesterday. Well, friends, this does not work. This ain't going to make you *happy*, and it ain't going to make you *strong*, and it ain't going to build a *Union*, and there's no way in the *world* it will. No sir. You don't get strong unless you do the work yourself . . . it's the same if you're down at the *face*, and it's the same if you're on a picket line. Brothers, here's how you get strong: (*Espies* CLORIS.) Evening, Cloris.

CLORIS: Evening, Timmy.

(*The* MINERS, *severally, say hello to* CLORIS, *she acknowledges them.*)

TIMMY (*to* CLORIS): Where was I?

CLORIS: Right before "You get strong if you *are* strong."

TIMMY: Thank you. (*To* MINERS:) Friends, you get strong if you *are* strong . . . (*To* CLORIS): Who's your friend?

ALBERT: Albert Litko, I got locked in.

CLORIS: I'm getting him out.

TIMMY (*confidentially, to* CLORIS): Nice lookin' fella.

CLORIS: Not bad.

TIMMY (*To* ALBERT): Timmy O'Shea.

ALBERT: Pleased to meet you.

(*They shake hands.*)

TIMMY: Rest of the group: Lars Svenson, Bo Lund, Stosh Zabisco . . . feller in the funny hat's named Harry.

HARRY: Hiya, Pal.

ALBERT: Hi.

TIMMY (*to* ALBERT): Why don't you sit *down* a minute. Holdin' a meeting.

ALBERT: Well, thanks, but we're kind of . . . uh, what Union do you work for?

TIMMY: Don't work for any union. *Used* to work for the U.M.W. of A. Now, I'm on a pension, same's these fellas here. Siddown. (*To* MINERS:) Friends:

ALBERT: Do you guys actually mine coal in here?

TIMMY: Nope. All show. Miners're real, though.

STOSH: Goddamn right.

TIMMY: Known Stosh all my life. Grew up together.

ALBERT: And he never joined the Union?

STOSH: Joined the Union 1928. Mass Meeting. John L. on the Dais. Never forget it. Fought all m'life. Dug, fought . . .

ALBERT: You're a Union member?

BO: Ve vas *all* Union.

ALBERT: But, then, what's the lecture for?

TIMMY: Pass the time . . . old times . . . bringing back old times. Just passing the time . . .

BO: Ve vas *all* in de Union.

ALBERT: And, uh, what do you do in the Museum now?

TIMMY: Reminisce.

ALBERT: Ah.

TIMMY: Yup.

HARRY: We're doin' a little reminiscin'. Ain't been inside a mine, 1952. 'Tober fourth, 1952. Worked 21 years in the mines.

(TIMMY *starts to sing "The Song of the Thirties." The song of the depression, the little steel strike, and violent labor troubles, Ethiopia, Spain, the Lincoln Brigade.*)

Yup. Had things happen to me you wouldn't believe. Seen things *I* didn't believe. West Virginia . . . Pennsylvania . . . spent sixty-two hours once in a four-foot seam . . .

(*The* MINERS *join* TIMMY *in song.*)

LARS: Feller must share de action and excitement of his time, on pain of having been judged not to have lived. Oliver Vendell Holmes, a great American.

TIMMY (*to* ALBERT): What do *you* do?

ALBERT: Well, I'm out of work right now.

HARRY: No shame in that.

ALBERT: No.

HARRY: Might as well be, though, huh?

ALBERT: Yes.

TIMMY: You know anything about organizing? I like the way you look.

ALBERT: Well, no, I uh . . . I'm *flattered* but . . . I really should be getting . . . home.

TIMMY: Wide-open *field* . . .

ALBERT: Uh, no, I uh . . . I mean, my father was a Republican.

HARRY: He outta work?

TIMMY: Well, if you ever change your *mind* . . .

ALBERT: Yes. Thank you. Thank you very much.

(*A tableau. Both groups, obviously taken with each other, are loathe to part.*)

Well I guess we really should be getting on.

(ALBERT *and* CLORIS *start to walk away.*)

HARRY: You take it easy now, Brother.

ALBERT: You, too, it's a pleasure to have met you.

(*As they walk away the voice of* TIMMY *haranguing the* MINERS *can be heard.* TIMMY *shouts after* CLORIS.)

TIMMY: Cloris, where was I?

CLORIS: "The way to get strong is to be strong."

TIMMY: Right. (*To* MINERS:) The way to get strong is to *be* strong. Country wasn't founded by a bunch of sissies: "What's in this for *me*" . . . founded by a bunch of men and women not afraid to take a chance . . . (*His voice fades out.*)

ALBERT: What nice guys.

CLORIS: You said it.

ALBERT: And you support them, huh?

CLORIS: They support us.

(*Their stroll takes them through the turn-of-the-century street.*)

'Member you got a boomerang thrown at you?

ALBERT: Yes. I do.

CLORIS: Potawatamies. Neo-Potawatamies. Bunch of nowhere creeps. Trying to knock off Rudy.

ALBERT: Why?

CLORIS: For his pension check. Everybody in here lives off the pension checks of the old folks.

ALBERT: Oh.

CLORIS: So prices go up and Pierre and his Neo-Potawatamies come up with the bright idea that if we whack out the old folks and take their checks, there's more food for the lot of us.

ALBERT: That's terrible.

CLORIS: The terrible thing is that Pierre has been talking with John and the Farmers, trying to get their help getting rid of the old folks . . .

ALBERT: (Senior citizens.)

CLORIS: (We just call 'em old folks) . . . and John is starting to come around.

ALBERT: No.

CLORIS: Yes. Pierre comes in there with all this garbage about Survival of the Fittest, Natural Selection, The Law of Life, and so on, and the Farmers listen. (You can convince an intellectual of anything, ever notice that?) (*Pause.*) It's terrible. I mean, growing old is no joke . . .

ALBERT: No . . .

CLORIS: But it's not a *crime,* huh? How you going to beat Entropy? It's a surefire losing proposition. (*Pause.*) Had a guy used to live here, used to be the office boy for Robert Todd Lincoln. Used to tell us stories Robert Todd told him, his father told him. I mean, we're talking about the transmission of infor*ma*tion, here.

ALBERT: Yes.

CLORIS: I mean, we're talking about *real* history here. (You don't get close with the old people, who's going to tell you about life, Nevins and Commager?) What are you going to do when *you* get up there, jump off a building? It's very adolescent.

ALBERT: Uh huh.

CLORIS: Best goddamn organizer in the Country. John L. treated him like a son. *I'm* glad to have him here. (Sonofagun knows a lot of *songs*.) Goddamn Potawatamies should be ashamed of themselves. What kind of a society is frightened of its history? (*Pause.*)

ALBERT: I like the way you talk.

(CLORIS *shrugs.*)

I like it a lot. You impress me. Would you like to come home with me?

CLORIS: I live *here.* And besides I hardly know you.

ALBERT: Oh. (*Pause.*) It's been a very rough day.

CLORIS: That doesn't necessarily mean that I should go to bed with you.

ALBERT: No, you're right. I got stood up.

CLORIS: I'm sorry.

ALBERT: I like the way you look.

CLORIS: I'm glad. (*Pause.*)

(ALBERT *sings the sad song of* "The Myth of Free Love and the Myth and Reality of Promiscuity." CLORIS *joins him. At the end of the song there is a long pause. The two look at each other.* DIETER, *a wizened man in a somewhat military-looking fatigue costume approaches. He is in his sixties.*)

DIETER: *Guten abend.*

CLORIS: *N'abend.*

ALBERT: *N'abend.*

(*Pause.*)

DIETER: Someone srew a boomerang at me.

CLORIS: They're starting.

DIETER: Zis is terrible. Terrible.

CLORIS: I know it.

DIETER: Somesing must be done.

CLORIS: The question is but what. (*To* ALBERT:) This is Dieter Gross.

ALBERT: Albert Litko.

DIETER: Enchanted.

CLORIS: He got locked inside.

DIETER: He didn't.

ALBERT: Yes, I did.

DIETER: That is too bad.

CLORIS: Dieter used to work on the U-505 submarine.

ALBERT: Yes? What, as a janitor?

DIETER: No, I vas radioman and forvard damage control. (*Pause.*)

ALBERT: When did you work on it?

DIETER: Sirty-nine srough forty-sree.

ALBERT: Oh.

DIETER: I vent home on leave, I get sick, I am separated from ze ship.

ALBERT: Oh.

DIETER: I rejoin ze ship in 1959 as Janitor at her present moorings in Chicago. In 1964 I am retired, and now I just hang out.

(ALBERT *nods.*)

CLORIS: Show him your medal, Dieter.

DIETER: Nooo.

CLORIS: Go on.

(DIETER *grudgingly and ceremoniously takes a felt pouch from his clothing, and removes a medal from it, which he shows to* ALBERT.)

ALBERT: What . . . what is it for?

DIETER: Oh, nosing special. Ze North-Atlantic. Forty-one. Nosing Special.

CLORIS: It's the Iron Cross.

DIETER: I von it on dat ship. (*Points toward submarine. Pause.*)

ALBERT: And now you just hang out here?

DIETER: Ya. I like it here. You like it here?

ALBERT: Well, uh, yes.

DIETER: I like it here. It has some assmosphere, ya?

ALBERT: Yes.

DIETER: It has some . . . *weight.* Zis building is a Monument to Science.

ALBERT: Yes.

DIETER: Zis building is a Monument to Orderly Understanding, and a Stark Affront to all ze ravages of Time.

CLORIS: You think so, Dieter?

DIETER: Ya, I sink so, else I vould not live here. (I live here out of choice) . . .

ALBERT: . . . uh-huh . . .

DIETER: . . . to be close to ze ship I love . . . of course . . . and out of respect for ze larger principles on which ziz building stands.

(DIETER *sings the song of his attempts to find "A Reasonable Life." He sings of his youth in Germany, of the Depression, of the Nazis, of his life in the navy, of the end of the war. At the end of his song he turns to* ALBERT.)

So, you are locked in here, eh?

ALBERT: Yes, I . . . I'm on my way out.

DIETER: Hmmm. You know Szoreau? Szoreau is in jail, Emerson comes to visit him. Emerson says "Szoreau, vat are you doing in a Museum?," Szoreau says, "Ralph, what are you doing *not* in a Museum." Ziz is how I feel.

ALBERT: But I have to get home.

(DIETER *nods. The air is rent by the screams of the* POTAWATAMIES. *The camera peeks over the second level balcony to reveal the* POTAWATAMIES, paunchy types in Glaneagles raincoats, herding the MINERS *with spears.*)

CLORIS (*shouting*): Pierre, you sonofabitch, you leave those men alone.

TIMMY (*shouting up*): We're alright, Honey.

(TIMMY *gets whacked on the head with a spear.*)

CLORIS (*sotto voce*): FUCKING CREEPS. (*To* ALBERT:) Come on, we gotta do something.

DIETER: I go for help to ze *landsmenschen.*

CLORIS: Good luck.

(DIETER *goes for help.*)

CLORIS (*shouting*): Dammit, Pierre, you leave those guys alone.

(CLORIS, *with* ALBERT *in tow, runs down the stairs and after the* PO-TAWATAMIES. *A chase throughout the museum. A reprise of "The Song of the*

Thirties" [as it would be sung by the Soviet Army Men's Chorus] is in the
background. The chase takes them through a large part of the museum and
culminates in a remote part of the first floor, where CLORIS *and* ALBERT
encounter PIERRE *and his* POTAWATAMIES *about to do harm to the* MINERS.)

CLORIS: Okay, Pierre, give it up.

PIERRE: This is just *dialectic*, Cloris, this is the Law of life.

CLORIS: I'll *give* you the Law of life, Pierre, pick on someone your own
age, for Chrissakes.

PIERRE: It's not for nothing that we're younger than they are . . .

CLORIS: No?

PIERRE: There's a plan in this.

CLORIS: This is strongarm and robbery.

PIERRE: That's a very limited view, Cloris.

CLORIS: Well, you just let 'em alone.

PIERRE: Or you are gonna what?

(*The shouts of* DIETER *are heard.*)

CLORIS (*shouting*): Dieter! We're over here. Now you're gonna get
yours, creep.

(DIETER *appears with the* FARMERS *behind him.*)

CLORIS (*to* JOHN): Al*right* alright alright. And about time, too.
(Thank God.)

JOHN: What, uh, seems to be the trouble here?

PIERRE: Hi, John.

JOHN: Pierre.

CLORIS: They want to whack out the miners.

JOHN (*to* PIERRE): This true?

PIERRE: Yes. (*Pause.*)

JOHN: You don't, uh, really want to do that, do you, Pierre?

PIERRE: Yes.

JOHN: But, why?

PIERRE: Money.

(*A pause.* PIERRE *and the* POTAWATAMIES *advance on the* MINERS *brandishing blunt instruments.*)

TIMMY (*to* MINERS): Sing, boys!

(MINERS *break into "Solidarity Forever," which continues behind ensuing dialogue.*)

CLORIS: You hold it right for Chrissake there, Pierre. John. John . . .

(JOHN *starts surreptitiously edging away from scene of conflict.*)

CLORIS: John, where are you going?

JOHN: Going? I'm not going anywhere.

CLORIS: Then why are you getting farther away? (*Pause.*) John? John where are you going? (*Pause.*) You can't do this, John. You come back here. You come *back* here. (CLORIS *interposes self between* POTAWATAMIES *and* MINERS. *To* FARMERS:) Douggie, Fran, Bruce, where do you think you're going with him?

JOHN: We have a social function to fulfill, Cloris, which does not encompass getting hit on the head. This is a struggle for property between two naturally opposed groups, and the intervention of our faction would be the sheerest *gaucherie.* (*Pause.*) White-collar liberalism. (*Pause.*) These people are much closer to the roots of the problem than we, Cloris. There are variables in this conflict whose *existence* we are not even aware of. (*Pause.*) The urge to acquire property is a primordial and (we may assume) in the final analysis, a *constructive* urge. (*Pause. Summoning* FARMERS:) Friends . . .

(RUDY *separates self from* FARMERS *and stands with* CLORIS.)

RUDY: That is the *lowes'* bunch of verbige I ever *did* hear. You come back here, John.

JOHN: I have a responsibility to these people (*indicating* FARMERS. *A* POTAWATAMIE *advances on a* MINER.)

POTAWATAMIE: Gimme your wallet, Gramps.

ALBERT (*to* POTAWATAMIE): Okay, okay, this has gone about far enough. Here's what we're going to do . . .

(ALBERT *gets whacked across the head with a quarterstaff. He falters.*)

CLORIS: John, I swear to God . . . you come back here.

JOHN (*reverting to a childish tone*): If they're so smart, how come they're old?

ALBERT (*to* POTAWATAMIE): Why don't you put down those things and go home?

POTAWATAMIE: We live here.

CLORIS (*to* JOHN): If *you're* so smart, how come you're living in a museum on Twinkies?

JOHN (*incensed*): What did you say?

CLORIS: You heard me.

(JOHN *screams, and runs at* CLORIS. *The* POTAWATAMIES, *sensing their bloodlust condoned, turn on the* MINERS *in force.* ALBERT *interjects self into the fray.*)

ALBERT: You leave these folks alone, you goons. (*He gets another whack in the head.*)

(*A major fight.* RUDY *is seen fighting bravely.* CLORIS *and* ALBERT *gravitate toward each other in the fray.*)

POTAWATAMIE (*eerily*): Youth is Nature's Gift to the Young!!

(*The* MINERS *continue to sing. Suddenly, the tide of battle turns so that* MINERS, RUDY, CLORIS, *and* ALBERT *find themselves in a cul-de-sac. The* POTAWATAMIES *and the* FARMERS *control the exit. All, sensing the imminence of the end, fall silent. A pause. The* POTAWATAMIES *and the* FARMERS *close in on the opposing faction.* ALBERT *unconsciously slips his arm around* CLORIS. *A pause.*)

CLORIS: John, you . . .

JOHN (*cutting her off*): Sticks and stones will break my bones, but names will never hurt me. (*Pause.*)

PIERRE (*a battlecry*): "Let's hear it for *now*!!!!"

(*All the* POTAWATAMIES *scream and run at the three friends. In their charge* ALBERT *finds himself thrust against a firedoor, which opens with his weight, and he finds himself outside the museum in an early dawn. The sounds of screaming continue within the museum.* ALBERT *pounds on the door, but his pounding is not answered.*)

ALBERT (*screaming*): Let me in. Let me in.

(*He begins to run around the museum from entrance to entrance, trying all the doors in an attempt to get in. Running around the back he trips over a pair of lovers, and says "Sorry," and continues running. His run finally takes him to the main* {*north*} *entrance, where we see him trying the doors. We hear someone shouting at him from the entrance drive.*)

POLICEMAN: Hey. Hey. Hey, you . . .

(ALBERT *turns and we see that he is being shouted at by a* POLICEMAN *in a patrol car.*)

The Museum doesn't open for four hours. (*To his companion officer:*) I never *seen* this.

(ALBERT *turns back to the main door and continues to pound and cry* "Let me in.")

(*His* COMPANION OFFICER, *who is sleeping with his hat over his eyes, answers him.*)

SECOND POLICEMAN: What?

POLICEMAN: I don't know . . . some kind of *culture* junkie, something . . . (*To* ALBERT:) Go home, go read a book, something.

(ALBERT *does not move.*)

Did you *hear* me? I said move on.

(*Pause.* ALBERT *reluctantly starts to walk down the stairs.*)

Okay.

(*The patrol car pulls away.* ALBERT *walks sadly down the stairs. As he walks down the stairs, a yellow schoolbus pulls up. It has about fifty Shriners in full dress regalia in it. The Shriners file out of the bus and set up on the stairs to have a formal group picture taken by a fellow with an old bellows camera and flash pan. Shooting down from the roof of the museum we see the Shriners assembled,* ALBERT *trudging toward the lone car in the parking lot [A 1963 Dodge Dart]. The flash pan goes off, the Shriners file back into the schoolbus, which pulls away, leaving* ALBERT *alone in the parking lot, trudging to his car. A helicopter shot of* ALBERT *going to his car and a voice over of a traffic report.*)

TRAFFIC REPORT: . . . smooth right up to the Junction. Eden's a little heavy between Armitage and Congress, and the Ryan, as usual, backed up from the Loop to 95th Street. And now back to Jim.

JIM THE DISC JOCKEY: Thank you. Bob, we'll have another report in fifteen, but here's one we've got a *lot* of requests for, and we're sending this out to Doug from Betty.

(*The radio plays the closing song, "The Museum of Science and Industry Story." The helicopter follows* ALBERT'*s car into South Shore Drive and traffic as he heads north. Credits super.*)

A Wasted Weekend

Dramatis Personae

RADIO ANNOUNCER
JABLONSKI
RENKO
HILL
LUCY BATES
BUNTZ
HENRY GOLDBLUME
BELKER
KHAKI OFFICER
HUNTER
FURRILLO
STATE TROOPER
SECOND STATE TROOPER
YOUNG WOMAN (MISS CARRINGTON)
GUY
I.A.D. OFFICER
LAWYER
PROPRIETOR OF THE CURRENCY EXCHANGE
ROBBER
OFFICER

INTERIOR: JABLONSKI'S HOUSE. DAY.

(*Angle: Kitchen countertop. Man in plaid lumberjack shirt making coffee.*)

RADIO ANNOUNCER (*voice over*): I'll be with you this morning right up until six a.m., Roger Armandale and the traffic report. Thanks for stickin' with me through the night. If you've *been* up all night, here is the song for you. For those of you who just got up, here's how the other half lives: the immortal Glenn Miller:

(*Radio starts playing "Moonlight Serenade."*)

(*Hand comes into the frame, picks up a clock, it reads 4:45. Sound of a knock on the door.*)

(*Angle:* JABLONSKI, *the man in the lumberjack shirt, going to open the back door.* HILL *and* RENKO *enter. They are dressed in outdoorsy clothes. They come into the kitchen and make themselves comfortable at the kitchen table.*)

RENKO: Oh yes, oh yes, oh yes.

HILL: *Gimme* some of that coffee . . .

(JABLONSKI *starts pouring them coffee.*)

JABLONSKI: How'd you sleep last night?

HILL: Not a wink, man, I was up at *two*, at *three* . . .

RENKO: I couldn't sleep . . . I was up cleaning my *gear, packing* . . .

HILL: . . . where's Henry?

JABLONSKI: . . . meeting him at the Stationhouse.

RENKO: . . . maan, I'm thinkin' . . . get me out of that car and get me out of that *job* a minute, get me somewhere where it *matters* . . .

HILL (*gets up, holding his coffeecup, checks his watch*): Come on, we'll take it in the car.

(RENKO *gets up.* JABLONSKI *puts on his coat. They all move toward the door.* JABLONSKI *takes several hunting rifles from behind the door, passes them out to his friends. As* RENKO *exits he declaims:*)

RENKO: "My heart's in the highlands. My heart is not here. My heart's in the highlands a chasin' the deer."

(*They exit the kitchen. We hear them faintly, outside, talking.*)

INTERIOR: SQUAD ROOM

Roll call. LUCY BATES *in charge.*

BATES: Lieutenant will be posting the duty roster for the next rotation . . . (*checks clipboard*) . . . those of you interested, your requests for overtime . . .

(*Reaction:* "Yeah. What about 'em . . . ?")

BATES: They're in process. Several of them have been submitted for the Pulitzer Prize for Modern Fiction . . . (*Checks list. Holds up a composite drawing.*) White man, early thirties, shoulder-length blond hair, blue windbreaker . . . this is the *third* armed robbery, a currency exchange, last night. Eighteenth and Promontory. *Look* for him. White male, one hundred fifty pounds, medium height, shoulder-length blond hair, a blue windbreaker . . . (*She lowers the composite drawing, checks her list.*) Ther'll be a bunch of Boy Scouts in the House today. The Captain's talking to them at eleven hundred hours on "Law Enforcement as a Career." Anyone who'd like to attend is . . .

BUNTZ: Law Enforcement as a *Hobby* . . . ?

BATES: In your case I see how that's appropriate, but the Captain's subject will be Law Enforcement as a Career . . .

(HENRY GOLDBLUME *comes up to the podium, dressed in hunting clothes. He hands a sheaf of papers to* BATES.)

Thank you, Lieutenant.

(GOLDBLUME *nods, obviously in a hurry.*)

. . . the Captain's looking for you.

GOLDBLUME: Where is he . . . ?

BATES: His office.

(GOLDBLUME *nods, hurries off.* BATES *checks her clipboard.*)

I would like you all to read and pay attention to the recommendations regarding the carrying of a second or back-up gun. The registration and permission must be in your file. The registration and permission must be in your file, and you must qualify with this gun as well as your service revolver at the range. We recommend the back-up gun and we recommend *practice;* the life you save may be your own. Any questions?

BELKER: Why is Lieutenant Goldblume going undercover?

BATES: The Lieutenant is not going undercover. For those of you who've kept pace with developments in your community, the Lieutenant and several of your colleagues are going out to kill Bambi. They are going *hunting*. They are going out to slaughter poor defenseless creatures . . .

BUNTZ: . . . if you can eat it, you can kill it.

BATES: Officer Buntz can keep the details of his personal life to himself . . . (*checks clipboard*) . . . alright . . . the new rotation figures on the board . . . thank you for your attention.

(*The roll call starts to break up.* BUNTZ *walks by the podium.*)

BATES (to BUNTZ): How can you defend him? Killing poor deer just to prove his "Manhood"?

BUNTZ: 'Least he's got one.

BATES: I expected no less. Have a nice day.

INTERIOR: SQUAD ROOM, IMMEDIATELY FOLLOWING.

GOLDBLUME *walking through the squad room. A* KHAKI OFFICER *calls after him.*

KHAKI OFFICER: Lieutenant, I need you to sign off on those Robbery Reports . . .

GOLDBLUME: No. No. No. NO. I'm not *here* today. It's an illusion.

KHAKI OFFICER: . . . take five minutes . . .

GOLDBLUME: Nope. Nope. I'm gonna talk to the Captain, and I'll see you at the end of the week.

(*He walks past* HUNTER, *who declaims:*)

HUNTER: "And Nimrod was a Mighty Hunter in the Land . . ."

(JABLONSKI, HILL, *and* RENKO *enter. Camera follows* GOLDBLUME *as he walks over to them.* JABLONSKI *is calling back over his shoulder.*)

JABLONSKI: . . . round the corner, get the car filled . . .

RENKO: . . . anyone like to contribute. Let's get the kitty started. Lieutenant . . . ?

(GOLDBLUME *goes into his pocket. Takes out money in a moneyclip, throws it to* RENKO.)

RENKO: Thank *you,* sir. Right back . . .

(RENKO *exits.*)

GOLDBLUME: I've got to have two words with the Captain . . .

(GOLDBLUME *walks over to the captain's office.* JABLONSKI *calls after him.*)

JABLONSKI: Quickly as you can, Sir. We've got to pick up the keys to the Hunting Lodge . . .

(LUCY BATES *comes over to the desk at which we find* HUNTER, JABLONSKI, *and* HILL.)

HUNTER (*to* BATES, *gesturing at the deerhunters*): . . . an interesting ceremony.

BATES: What is?

HUNTER: Hunting.

BATES: *Is* it?

HUNTER: Bonding, the Letting of Blood . . .

BATES: Oh. Everybody with their Secrets. Boys' Clubs. No Girls Allowed . . .

HILL: You want to come, Sarge?

BATES: No. No, thank you.

(She starts to walk out of the shot.)

HILL: Then what do you care . . . ?

(She turns back.)

BATES: I care because defenseless creatures will be killed.

JABLONSKI *(of* HILL): Not the way *he* shoots . . . *I* saw you sighting in that rifle!!!

BATES *(comes back)*: Well, I think it's *disgusting* . . .

HILL: Then you go eat *beansprouts* the rest of your life!

BATES: Oh. "If I can Eat it I can Kill it." Well. I don't *eat* deer.

HILL: That's right, you don't eat deer. 'Cause, you want to eat *deer,* you have to go up there and *stalk* the sucker . . . you have to . . .

INTERIOR: FURRILLO'S OFFICE.

FURRILLO *behind the desk, talking to* GOLDBLUME.

GOLDBLUME: *What?*

FURRILLO: If there were some way out of it, Henry, I'd take that way.

GOLDBLUME: Sir, it's just an accident that I'm *in* here today. I have two days off, and I just stopped in to drop off the Rotation Rosters.

FURRILLO: I know, and I . . . Henry, I won't order you to do it. But I'm called *downtown,* and there are going to be twenty-five Boy Scouts here expecting a lecture. And someone has to do it. You'll be done by eleven thirty.

GOLDBLUME: . . . the men are waiting in the car.

FURRILLO: Can't you drive up and meet them? (*Beat.*) Henry?

GOLDBLUME: Yessir.

FURRILLO: Thank you. Thank you very much.

(KHAKI OFFICER *knocks on the door and beckons the captain.*)

KHAKI OFFICER: Captain . . . ???

FURRILLO: I'm coming. Thank you, Henry.

INTERIOR: DESK AREA, SQUAD ROOM.

BATES *et al, still arguing.*

HUNTER: Because the Personification of Animals, as done by Walt

Disney . . . talking *deer,* cute *rabbits,* I suggest if you *study* the actions of all Animals in the Wild . . .

BATES: Well, yes, well, let *them* even out the Balance of Nature, 'cause it's not our job.

(RENKO *enters.*)

RENKO: Alright. Gassed up and ready to roll, *let* us roll . . .

(GOLDBLUME *comes out of the captain's office.*)

JABLONSKI: Lieutenant Goldblume. Here we go.

GOLDBLUME: I'm not going. I'll have to meet you there. (*Beat.*) I'm going to be tied up here 'til eleven thirty. I'll drive up and meet you there. (*Beat.*) I'm just . . . I'm just . . . I'll *meet* you there.

(JABLONSKI *shrugs, takes out a pencil, makes a map on a sheet of paper.*)

JABLONSKI: You get off of 201. Go east two miles to the Corner Store. You take a left. Four or five miles you will see a yellow house with a red barn on the right. You take the next dirt road to the right. You can't miss it . . .

(FURRILLO, *putting on his coat, walks through the shot.*)

FURRILLO: I'm sorry, Henry. I'll make it up to you.

RENKO (*to* GOLDBLUME): We'd stay, but we've got to get the keys . . .

GOLDBLUME: No, no, no, that's alright. I'll meet you there.

(JABLONSKI, RENKO, *and* HILL *exit leaving* HUNTER, BATES, *and* GOLDBLUME *by the desk. Beat.*)

HUNTER: "I slept and dreamt that life was Beauty
I woke and found that life was Duty." (*He meditates on this a moment,
then leaves.*)

BATES (*to* GOLDBLUME): Sir: long as you're here, you want to stalk the
wild Requests for Overtime with me?

(GOLDBLUME *sighs. Takes off his hunting coat. Picks up a sheaf of papers
and walks through the squad room alongside* BATES. BUNTZ *passes from the
other direction.*)

BUNTZ (*to* GOLDBLUME): Nothing like a Day in the Woods . . . huh?

INTERIOR: PARKED STATION WAGON. DAY.

HILL *and* RENKO *sitting in the front seat. The car parked by a highway
diner.* RENKO *studying a spread-out road map. He senses* HILL *looking at
something, looks up from the map.*

RENKO: What?

HILL (*gesturing with his head toward another car*): Blue pickup, Michigan Plates.

RENKO (*looking*): What about it?

HILL: Think we had the plates on the *Hot* list.

(RENKO *looks hard at the car.*)

RENKO (*relaxes*): Wrong car. Put it in *neutral,* my friend. Let yourself
kick back. Now, you say to yourself: A Man Who is Only His Job . . .
what is he? A *machine.* Not even a machine. A *cog* in a machine. We
were not put on this earth just to *work.* The word is "recreation."

Recreation. *Meditate* on that a second. 'Til roll call on Monday morning, we are not Cops, but *Men*. Men in the Country . . .

(JABLONSKI *gets into the backseat, holding a paper sack, starts distributing foodstuffs.*)

RENKO: Gimme a sandwich . . .

HILL: Coffee.

JABLONSKI: You guys think about the problem?

HILL: I did.

JABLONSKI: Tell me.

HILL: Deer breaks cover, runs to the crest of a ridge. We . . .

JABLONSKI: . . . yes . . .

HILL: Lay low.

RENKO: Well, that's obvious.

HILL: . . . unmoving. Wait 'til the deer's had the time to . . .

JABLONSKI: Right. No. That is what we do *not* want to do. The deer breaks cover, runs to the crest, *you've* got the advantage.

HILL: Because?

(JABLONSKI *takes a sandwich, a couple of pencils, and acts out the tableau on the dashboard, the sandwich representing the deer, the pencils representing the hunters.*)

JABLONSKI: 'Cause he can't *hear* you. He's running too hard. The deer's heart is pounding, he's *terrified*, his perceptions are dull. For one moment he's playing *your* game. The deer's running to the ridge, the thing to do, *you* run to the ridge. Odds are you're going to get a shot at him when he comes up the other side. Another thing:

RENKO (*of sandwich*): Oooh, this stuff's good . . .

JABLONSKI: A deer breaks cover on the *flat* . . .

RENKO: Now: where are we . . . ?

(*Angle insert: The tableau on the dashboard,* JABLONSKI *manipulating the pencils.*)

JABLONSKI (*voice over*): Let's say we're in the brush, here and here . . .

(*We hear a commanding male voice.*)

MALE VOICE (*offscreen*): Please put your hands on the dashboard, man in the backseat, put your hands on the back of the seat in front of you.

(*Angle: Two* STATE TROOPERS *flanking the car, the men inside the car.*)

JABLONSKI: Uh, we're . . .

STATE TROOPER: Please do as I say. Right now, please . . .

RENKO: Umh, we're *police* officers . . .

STATE TROOPER: Right now. Please. *Right* now . . .

INTERIOR: SQUAD ROOM. DAY.

GOLDBLUME, *dropping off some sheets on* BATES' *desk.*

BATES: Thank you, Sir.

GOLDBLUME: My pleasure.

(*Camera follows* GOLDBLUME *out through the squad room.* HUNTER *attaches himself to him.*)

HUNTER: I find that an unfortunate aspect of our society is the absence of alternative means of establishing status.

GOLDBLUME: Uh huh.

HUNTER: *Yes.* There is a certain status-structure in any job, who is boss, who is an *underling.* And too-close *adherence* to that structure causes *jealousy* of those above, *envy* of those below. Which is why, the Company *baseball* team . . .

GOLDBLUME (*trying to extricate himself*): I've got to write a talk . . .

HUNTER: Well, let me make this point, you see: I think the fact that you are going *hunting* with the men below you, while some might say, is a violation of the status-structure, is, in fact . . .

GOLDBLUME: I've got to talk to twenty-five Boy Scouts in a half an hour . . .

HUNTER: Oh.

(*As* GOLDBLUME *walks by the desk, the* KHAKI OFFICER *calls his attention to a very beautiful woman around thirty, who has obviously just filed a complaint.*)

GOLDBLUME: Yes . . . ?

KHAKI OFFICER: We, would you talk to this woman please . . . ?

GOLDBLUME: I'm Lieutenant Goldblume, I'm in the midst of . . .

KHAKI OFFICER: If you just have five minutes, Sir . . .

(GOLDBLUME *sighs. The camera follows the* YOUNG WOMAN *and* GOLD-BLUME *into his office.*)

INTERIOR: THE OFFICE.

YOUNG WOMAN *sits down.*

GOLDBLUME: Miss . . . ?

YOUNG WOMAN: Carrington.

GOLDBLUME: Miss Carrington. I have about (*checks watch*) five min-utes, if you . . .

YOUNG WOMAN: I'll be brief. I, uh . . . (*Beat.*) Many people are struck by the, uh, by the, by what happens in the cities, you, you think it will not affect *you.* You, people cannot stand the *stress,* and you look at people *around* you, and you see what happens to them and you say it won't happen to you . . . that . . . that . . .

GOLDBLUME: And what is your specific . . . ?

YOUNG WOMAN: My, my, my boyfriend won't make love to me . . .

INTERIOR: HIGHWAY DINER. DAY.

JABLONSKI, HILL, RENKO, *and one* STATE TROOPER *having coffee in a booth by the window.*

STATE TROOPER: . . . they said that the way to *do* it, they developed a drill . . .

RENKO: The *thing* of it, you should *never* give up the gun.

HILL: The statistics say never give up the gun.

STATE TROOPER: Well, that's what I'm *saying*. So they developed a drill . . .

JABLONSKI: I've *heard* of this . . .

STATE TROOPER: . . . you know what I'm talking about . . . ?

JABLONSKI: Man's got the drop on your partner, got your partner's gun. You work out a signal, call him by some . . .

STATE TROOPER: You call him by a strange name: you say, for example, "Clarence, give him what he wants." The word "Clarence" is the signal, he drops . . .

JABLONSKI: . . . your *partner* drops . . .

STATE TROOPER: Your partner hears *that* word, he drops to the ground, you draw and fire.

HILL: The chance that it's going to work . . . ?

RENKO: Well, man, the idea is, it's better to die on your *feet* . . .

(*The* SECOND STATE TROOPER *comes up to the table, slides in.*)

SECOND STATE TROOPER: . . . the word is: my cousin says, you work back from the *farmhouse,* three quarters mile back there is an old abandoned *apple* orchard, and that's where he took his deer last year.

HILL: Hey, man, we appreciate it.

SECOND STATE TROOPER: . . . pleasure.

(*The Hill Street Bunch start getting up from the table. The* STATE TROOPER *reaches for the check.*)

RENKO: No, it's on us. Thanks for the advice.

STATE TROOPER: *Thank* you.

HILL (*turns back*): And why'd you pull us over?

STATE TROOPER: Well, my partner thought you looked a tad "suspicious." *I* said, "they're just going to a *costume* party . . ."

RENKO: *Costume* party. These are our "Hunting Clothes . . ."

SECOND STATE TROOPER: Uh huh . . .

RENKO: . . . never hurts to show a little good *taste* in the woods . . .

JABLONSKI: Farmhouse, three quarters mile back, apple orchard . . .

HILL: Thanks for the advice.

STATE TROOPER: Always glad to help a fellow officer.

INTERIOR: SQUAD ROOM. DAY.

Twenty-five Boy Scouts in full regalia sitting expectantly.

(*Angle:* GOLDBLUME, *still in hunting clothes, holding notes. He makes another note in pencil, comes up to the podium. Sighs. Looks out at the Boy Scouts. Beat.*)

GOLDBLUME: My name is Henry Goldblume. I am a Lieutenant of the Metropolitan Police. It might look as if I am involved in some undercover mission, but I'm *dressed* like this for a simpler reason. It's my day off. (*He consults his notes.*) I am *speaking* to you today because you have expressed an interest in Law Enforcement as a career. Law Enforcement as a career. Now: what does this mean? It means many things. It means a career which offers . . . *friendship* . . . *loyalty*, from those around you and to those around you, and *pride* . . . (*Beat.*) *Service* . . . and, also, as I've been reminded here today, *duty*. And this is what I would like to say to you: Where does the pride come from? Where does the feeling of accomplishment come from? From *duty*. And *that* is the price that is exacted of you if you'd pursue and be happy in a career in the police. (*Beat.*)
How do you make the negative *positive*? How do you, how can you learn to take enjoyment in a job which is, which is for the most part *not* glamorous, but *repetitive*. Which involves paperwork, repetition, care . . . in which your accomplishments are not *dramatic* . . . ? When your job is standing on surveillance for twelve hours a day week after week . . . when you find the name you thought was the hot suspect died six months before the crime . . . when the case you worked a year on is thrown out of court . . . I'm speaking to you not as children now, but as men; because you have done us the compliment of coming here today to see the way we live . . . We are here to enforce the law. To serve and protect a populace in need of service and protection.

(*Angle: The back of the squad room.* BATES *and two other officers listening to the lecture, behind the Boy Scouts. Camera pans back to frame* HENRY GOLDBLUME, *as he continues to speak.*)

It is *their* will, the will of the people, expressed in the laws of the city, and the regulations of the department, that controls our life. The bad cop straining against that will, he bends the law, he flaunts the rules of the department, and his life in the force is an unhappy one—because this man forgoes the one, the *only* constant satisfaction he could have—the satisfaction of doing his duty. (GOLDBLUME *clears his throat, shifts down to the next page. He prepares to continue speaking.*)

EXTERIOR: LOG CABIN IN THE WOODS. DAY.

The station wagon. JABLONSKI *and* RENKO *by the front door, waiting.* HILL *comes around the back.*

HILL: All locked.

RENKO: Well, *dang* it all, man, why'd those Staties pull us over . . . ?

HILL (*to* JABLONSKI): Can we catch up with your guy, get the keys . . . ?

JABLONSKI: No, he's gone.

HILL: Where'd he, where would he usually *hide* the keys?

JABLONSKI: I don't know . . . this is my first time *here* . . .

HILL: You've never been here before?

JABLONSKI: The man's my landsman from the old days at Polk, he says "use my cabin" . . .

RENKO: Gentlemen: I think the *correct* answer here is: break in. (*Beat.*) We will break in. We will *unlock* the doors. Prior to leaving we will *seal* the window over with wood, and leave your friend ample funds to reglaze the window. (*To* JABLONSKI:) Your *sap,* please.

(JABLONSKI *hands him a sap.* RENKO *walks over to the house, breaks in a window, climbs in.*)

JABLONSKI: Now, the thing is: chop *wood* . . .

HILL: Chop wood. For . . . ?

JABLONSKI: For to heat the *house,* my friend, for we are in the *country* now.

(RENKO *opens the door of the cabin from the inside.* JABLONSKI *and* HILL *walk over to the front door.*)

RENKO: Well, your friend at Polk's doing some *well* for himself.

(*Camera follows* HILL *and* JABLONSKI *into the cabin which is sumptuously furnished with plush rugs, electronic equipment, heads of game. The men stand looking at it for a moment.*)

JABLONSKI: Well, we're just going to have to take the Bitter with the Better. Let's get unpacked.

HILL: Stan, does this mean no chopping wood . . . ?

(RENKO *settles down into a leather sofa.*)

RENKO: Man, I may not *go* hunting tomorrow. I may just stay here and order *up* a deer.

(JABLONSKI *closes the front door.*)

JABLONSKI: Well, break out the cards and let's get into this "*weekend*"!

INTERIOR: HILL STREET STATION. GOLDBLUME'S OFFICE.

He is tidying up some last minute papers. Hurrying into his hunting jacket.
BELKER *accosts him as he leaves.*

BELKER: Lieutenant.

GOLDBLUME: I am not here. I am going hunting . . .

BELKER: I was just going to wish you Good Shooting.

GOLDBLUME: Thank you.

(*Camera follows him out of his office and through the squad room as he mutters to himself.*)

GOLDBLUME (*sotto*): Eight hundred Boy Scouts . . . girl whose *boyfriend* won't make love to her . . . *overtime* . . .

(BUNTZ *calls to him across the squad room.*)

BUNTZ: You *shoot* 'em, Lieutenant, cause they'd do the same to you!!!

(GOLDBLUME *waves. He passes the front desk. Leaves some papers on the desk. As he goes out, the* YOUNG WOMAN *whose boyfriend would not make love to her enters. She points at* GOLDBLUME.)

YOUNG WOMAN: That's the man. That's the man that raped me.

(*Beat.* GOLDBLUME *sighs. Starts for the door.*)

He raped me in his office. I came here for *help*. I . . . is no one listening to me? I want to file a report!!!

(*The action in the squad room stops. Everyone turns to look at* GOLDBLUME. *Beat.* GOLDBLUME *starts taking off his hunting jacket. Comes back into the squad room.*)

INTERIOR: SUMPTUOUS HUNTING CABIN. EVENING.

Classical soft music on the stereo. A fire in the huge fieldstone fireplace. JABLONSKI, HILL, *and* RENKO *playing poker at a huge, oak-slab table.*

JABLONSKI: Two cards.

HILL (*dealing*): Two cards . . .

RENKO: *Similarly* . . .

HILL: Two cards for the man, and the dealer takes *one* . . .

RENKO: . . . frontin' off as usual.

HILL: And time will tell. And, Stan, I believe that it is your bet.

(*Sound of a key in the lock. All heads turn.*)

(*Angle point of view: The front door of the cabin opening. A man and a woman come in, necking furiously. Hold on the necking.*)

(*Angle: The men at the poker table, looking on.*)

(*Angle: The necking couple maneuvering themselves, entwined, toward the couch and the men at the table looking on for a long time. Finally* RENKO *clears his throat. He clears his throat again.*)

RENKO (*to* JABLONSKI): Is that your guy???

(JABLONSKI *shakes his head.*)

JABLONSKI: Sir . . . ?

(*The necking man looks up. Beat. He jumps back away from the disheveled, half-clothed woman. He starts dressing himself.*)

GUY: What are, you, who are, what you doing here . . . ?

(*The* GUY *starts trying to get a hunting rifle off of its moorings on the wall. The cops stand.*)

HILL: It's, it's, hold on, we're police officers . . . !!! HOLD IT!!! HOLD IT!!!

(JABLONSKI *and* HILL *are fumbling out their badges. The* GUY *continues to try to get the rifle off the wall.* RENKO *takes out his revolver and holds it up.*)

RENKO: I said hold it, for God's sake:

(*Beat. The* GUY *puts down the rifle.*)

Now, who are you?

GUY: Who are *you*?

JABLONSKI: We're friends of John Swoboda.

(*Beat.*)

GUY: And who is John Swoboda?

(*Beat.*)

HILL: Uh, is this John Swoboda's cabin?

GUY: No, it is not. It's *my* cabin.

HILL: And you are . . . ?

GUY: Who *I* am, it's none of your *business* who I am. You're in my home . . . what did, you're *police* officers . . . ???

RENKO: Yessir.

GUY: Well, then I think that you'd better give me your names and badge numbers.

JABLONSKI: Um, um, sir, could I *talk* to you a moment . . . could I talk with you a moment, please?

(JABLONSKI *goes off to the corner, leaving* RENKO, HILL, *and the disheveled young woman. Beat.*)

RENKO: We are *awful* sorry to have, as it seems we have, broken *in*to . . .

HILL: None of us have *been* here before, and we'll certainly . . .

RENKO: Any *damages* that . . .

JABLONSKI: Pack it up, lads, and let's move on. We want the next cabin down.

(HILL *and* RENKO *hurriedly assemble their belongings and apologize themselves out of the door.*)

HILL: We're incredibly sorry.

RENKO: An honest misunderstanding, any damages, we'll certainly . . .

(*Camera follows the three men out of the door, foodstuffs, rifles, hunting gear in their arms. They go over to the station wagon and they put their stuff in the station wagon. They start to drive down the dirt road.*)

HILL: How did you talk us out of that . . . ?

JABLONSKI: Guy had a wedding ring on, the woman did not. (*Beat.*)

RENKO: I *thought* he didn't kiss her like the two of them were married.

JABLONSKI: So it seems we're *all* of us going to forgive and forget.

HILL: So if we got the wrong place, then how is Henry going to find us?

RENKO: And where is *our* hunting lodge . . . ?

(*The car pulls up outside a hovel.*)

(*ANGLE EXTERIOR: THE HOVEL. Dark against the night sky. It is a falling down shack. The men get out.*)

JABLONSKI: Does anybody want to chop some wood . . . ?

INTERIOR: INTERROGATION ROOM. NIGHT.

GOLDBLUME, *still in hunting clothes. The* YOUNG WOMAN, *an* I.A.D. OFFICER, *a* LAWYER. GOLDBLUME *getting up from his seat.*

LAWYER: I'm very sorry.

GOLDBLUME: Not at all, not at all.

YOUNG WOMAN: I just don't know, I don't know what happened to my life . . .

(*She starts to cry.* GOLDBLUME, *the* I.A.D. OFFICER, *and the* LAWYER *exit.*)

LAWYER: I'm sorry to have emb . . .

GOLDBLUME: No, you didn't embarrass me . . . It's just . . .

LAWYER: I'm sure that nothing will come of it . . .

GOLDBLUME: Nothing will *come* of it? The woman's loonier than . . .

I.A.D. OFFICER: Lieutenant Goldblume was in a glass-walled room with this woman for something under five minutes. In *full* view of . . .

GOLDBLUME: Look: I'm on my day off.

(*He takes out his wallet. Takes out a card.*)

Whatever the thing is, let's talk about it, if we *have* to talk about it, next *week*.

I.A.D. OFFICER: Absolutely.

(*Shakes hands with* GOLDBLUME. GOLDBLUME *looks in his wallet.*)

GOLDBLUME: Oh hell . . .

(*We follow* GOLDBLUME *out into the squad room, looking at his wallet.*)

Can *anybody* lend me twenty dollars . . . ? Can . . . Well, let's not all rush up here at once. I'm on vacation, people, and I gave my money to Renko. I have no money for gas . . . (*He looks around. Sighs.*) Can anybody cash a *check* for me . . . ?

INTERIOR: RUN-DOWN HUNTING CABIN. NIGHT.

Interior of 10 × 12 barewood cabin. JABLONSKI *stoking up the small woodstove. The door opens and* HILL *comes in with an armful of wood. He deposits the wood on the floor next to* JABLONSKI, *takes off his coat.*

HILL: Working up a *chill* out there . . .

JABLONSKI: You think it's cold now? Wait 'til five a.m. out there!

(RENKO *is sitting at a table. He has his rifle disassembled and is cleaning it.* HILL *sits down at the table, takes his rifle out of the case and starts to break it down.* JABLONSKI *comes over with an enameled coffeepot. He pours coffee and sits down.*)

RENKO: Well, this is the life. *I* don't care, Henry, you are *missing* it . . .

HILL: Yeah. This is something more like *hunting* here!

RENKO (*to* JABLONSKI): Thank you.

(*They sit around cleaning their rifles and drinking the coffee.*)

Yep. This is *something*—more like it. (*Drinks coffee.*)

JABLONSKI: Don't want to drink *too* much of that.

HILL: Nope.

JABLONSKI: We want to hit the hay.

RENKO: Oh, yessir, be bright-eyed and bushy-tailed, four a.m., get the jump on some sleepy *deer* . . . (*Beat.*)

HILL: Funny how things come back.

RENKO: What is that?

HILL: Sitting around here, cleaning the rifle. (*Beat.*) Wood fire. (*Beat.*)

RENKO: Un-huh.

HILL: I remember, one time, sixty-nine. Seventy? We were, bunch of us were on a ridge about ten kilometers north of . . .

EXTERIOR: CURRENCY EXCHANGE. NIGHT.

GOLDBLUME *getting out of his car, walks into the currency exchange. Camera follows him in. Currency exchange is empty.* GOLDBLUME *goes up to the window.*

GOLDBLUME: Sir . . . Sir? I'd like to cash a check. Sir . . . (*Beat.*) Sir . . .

(*The* PROPRIETOR *comes over to the window.*)

GOLDBLUME: Sir, I'd like to cash a check.

PROPRIETOR: I, uh.

GOLDBLUME: I don't have an *account* here, but I'm a Police Officer . . . (*He takes out his badge.*)

PROPRIETOR: Oh, Thank God. Thank God. I've just, I'm waiting, I've just, I almost was held up.

GOLDBLUME: No.

PROPRIETOR: Yes, I uh . . .

GOLDBLUME: Look: did you call it in . . . ? What do you mean you were almost held up?

(*The* PROPRIETOR *holds up the circular we saw at roll call.*)

(*Angle: interior: circular.*)

(*Angle:* GOLDBLUME *and the* PROPRIETOR.)

PROPRIETOR: This circular, the bandit. He came in the store.

GOLDBLUME: How long ago was this?

PROPRIETOR: Ten minutes ago, he . . .

GOLDBLUME: He's gone by now. I'm sure the officers . . .

(*As he speaks two uniformed officers enter the currency exchange. The* PROPRI-
ETOR *starts to come out from behind the protective barrier.*)

GOLDBLUME: Sir, sir, if you could, before you, if you could just do me
the favor . . . (*He holds out his check.*)

EXTERIOR: CURRENCY EXCHANGE. NIGHT.

The squad car parked outside. GOLDBLUME, *happy, comes out of the currency
exchange hurrying. Camera tracks with him around the corner, to a dark
parking lot.* GOLDBLUME *gets happily into his car.*

(*Angle interior: Car. As* GOLDBLUME *starts the car, the driver's door is
wrenched open and the currency exchange* ROBBER *described in the circular
gets into the car and sticks a gun in* GOLDBLUME's *face.*)

ROBBER: Drive me out of here, and drive me out of here fast!

INTERIOR: RUN-DOWN CABIN. NIGHT.

The lamp is flickering low. JABLONSKI, HILL, *and* RENKO *huddled around
the table, talking quietly.*

JABLONSKI: . . . and we were, we'd been dropped into *Yugoslavia.*

HILL (*softly*): Uh-huh . . .

JABLONSKI: And we were *captured.*

HILL: I never knew that you were with the Airborne, Sarge.

JABLONSKI: Well, I was. And I don't know what it was. The pilot got it wrong, intelligence was wrong, but we ran into an advance unit of the German V Corps. (*Beat.*) And they, uh, there was some *talk* about it, there were *four* of us they caught, and they told us that they were going to . . . they'd tied us up, they were in a barn, it was an old horse barn. Stone. And we said what are you going to *do* with us. They said next day when they left, that they'd be taking us to, to their *base* camp as prisoners. They left us under the guard of this young kid, young kid, he was just a little younger than us. Must have been twenty. And the kid was . . . *he* knew they were going to kill us in the morning.

RENKO: They were going to kill you . . . ?

JABLONSKI: They were an advance unit of the Armored Corps. They weren't going to burden themselves with prisoners. (*Beat.*) And . . . well. And the kid, we appealed to him. Somebody, said one thing they'd like, as it was *obvious* that this was the last time that we'd ever have it, was we'd like a drink. The kid went up to the house. The Germans were staying in the house, and he brought back a bottle. (*Beat.*) We started to drink. (*Beat.*) And we got the kid drunk. And. Um . . . (*Beat.*) Well, you know, I'd *told* the story several times . . . as you do. It occurs to me that every time I told it I would say that we got the kid drunk and we slipped out. But the truth, the truth was, of course, we killed him. (*Beat.*)

HILL: Well. Somebody was going to have to die. Them or you.

JABLONSKI: Yes, that's true. And we knew it was true. (*Beat.*)

RENKO: Are you ever sorry that you killed him?

JABLONSKI: I'm sorry every day I live. (*Beat.*) But I wasn't going to let the man kill *me* . . .

HILL: Well.

JABLONSKI: Gentlemen: we're going hunting tomorrow. I think we should get some rest.

(JABLONSKI *blows out the lamp. The men settle back in their blankets.*)

JABLONSKI: Good night, men.

HILL: Good night, Sarge . . .

RENKO: Good night, Sarge.

INTERIOR: GOLDBLUME'S CAR.

GOLDBLUME *driving, the* ROBBER *still holding him at gunpoint.*

GOLDBLUME: I . . .

ROBBER: Just drive. Just keep on driving . . . (*The* ROBBER *looks in the backseat.*)

ROBBER: What is all that junk back there? (*Beat.*) I asked you a question.

GOLDBLUME (*pauses*): I'm going hunting.

ROBBER: *Hunting.*

(*Beat. The* ROBBER *takes out a cigarette. Looks for a match. Can't find one, starts patting down* GOLDBLUME. *Feels the gun underneath his jacket.*)

What is that??? What is that???

GOLDBLUME (*to himself*): Oh, my God . . .

ROBBER: What the hell is that??? (*He takes out* GOLDBLUME*'s revolver.*)

GOLDBLUME: I . . . (*Beat.*) I'm a police officer.

ROBBER: Oh. I got to pick a Cop. All the stuff that's already happened to me . . . oh man . . . oh man . . . pull the car over . . .

GOLDBLUME: Look.

ROBBER (*cocks the revolver*): I said pull over the car.

(*ANGLE EXTERIOR: THE CAR, ON AN ALREADY LONELY TWO-LANE BLACKTOP, PULLS OVER ONTO A DIRT ROAD.*)

(*Angle: The car struggling through the dirt lane. It stops.*)

ROBBER: Get out. (*Beat.*) I said get out. Take the keys.

(GOLDBLUME *gets out. The* ROBBER *goes around to the back of the car. He motions* GOLDBLUME *around to the back.*)

Open the trunk.

GOLDBLUME: I think we should talk about this.

ROBBER: I said open the trunk and when you open it then get in.

(*The trunk is opened. The* ROBBER *looks in.*)

No. No.

(*He takes out a shovel, throws it to* GOLDBLUME.)

Okay, you start digging.

(*Beat.* GOLDBLUME *looks at him.*)

GOLDBLUME: Please don't do this.

ROBBER: Dig a grave.

(*Beat.* GOLDBLUME *starts digging.*)

EXTERIOR: CABIN. DAWN.

RENKO *drinking from a metal can of orange juice. Standing next to* HILL, *both in full hunting clothes, blaze orange, daypacks on their backs, rifles over their shoulders. They are standing around a wood fire on the ground that is being tended by* JABLONSKI.

HILL (*of orange juice*): Gimme some of that . . .

(HILL *drinks from the can.* JABLONSKI *calls them over.*)

JABLONSKI: Okay. Stand in the woodsmoke. It's gonna hide any "city" scents that you have on you.

RENKO: Uh-huh . . .

JABLONSKI: Deer don't mind the smoke, but they'll run fifteen miles from the scent of After Shave.

RENKO: Well, some of us more *sartorial* ones *have* that problem . . .

(JABLONSKI *starts killing the fire.*)

JABLONSKI: That's enough.

(*He shovels earth on the fire.*)

RENKO (*to* HILL): Beautiful morning, huh?

HILL: You said it.

RENKO: Wish *Henry* was here . . .

JABLONSKI: Okay, let's move out. No talking in the woods.

RENKO: You got it.

(*The three men fan out and proceed slowly to a barbed-wire fence. They open the actions of their rifles and cross the fence. Close up their actions and proceed into the woods.*)

EXTERIOR: DIRT ROAD. DAWN.

The ROBBER *holding the gun on* GOLDBLUME, *who has just finished digging a shallow grave.*

ROBBER: Alright.

(GOLDBLUME *stops digging. Beat.*)

GOLDBLUME: And, and, and, that's it. Now you're going to kill me?

ROBBER: Oh, man, you know I *have* to kill you . . .

GOLDBLUME: You have to kill me?

ROBBER: Kidnapped a cop! Man . . . the climate in this state, that's
. . . you know that I have to kill you. They catch me, they're going to
kill *me, what* are you talking about?

GOLDBLUME: And what about if you didn't, if you *didn't* kidnap a cop.
They, I know who you are . . .

ROBBER: You know who I am.

GOLDBLUME: They want you for those *currency* exchange . . .

ROBBER: And what do you know about me?

GOLDBLUME: A description.

ROBBER: A description.

GOLDBLUME: We don't know your *name,* we . . .

ROBBER: What are you tellin' me . . . ?

GOLDBLUME: I'm telling you that no one has *anything.* They have an
M.O. You lay off, you *move* off, and I'm going to let this go.

ROBBER: You're going to let what go?

GOLDBLUME: I'm sposed to be hunting. No one knows where I am.
Nobody knows. Nobody saw me get into that car, No One Knows
Where I Am. If I go *back* tomorrow. I can go back, and this never
happened. You *take* the car. Take the car, take the . . . it has guns in
it, food, take it. I stopped by the road, I'll say I stopped, and you have
hours, "Someone stole my car." (*Beat.*) You hear what I'm saying?

ROBBER: I *kidnapped* you, man.

GOLDBLUME: *No* kidnapping. No. No . . . I Never Saw You. I saw you in a *lineup* I'd say . . . I never saw, I never saw this man before. You're a face on a circular. Look, look, look . . . what's in it for you? No kidnapping. No federal, no capital offense, you *know,* you know if you *do* this: you know they'll find you. I'm saying: Go Free: whatever it is that you want. That you want to do, you *do* it. I'm saying, all I'm saying: *leave* me here. I'm *begging* you. And something in it for *both* of us. You do what you want, but I'm saying . . . this, this, this is the right thing for us both.

ROBBER: You know that I can't believe you, man.

GOLDBLUME: It's the right *thing.* You know it is. Now you don't want to kill me. You want to . . . because you'd be killing us both. *Think* about you. I never saw you. I never saw you. (GOLDBLUME *sits down on the edge of the grave and hangs his head.*) I never saw you, this never happened, and you can go free, I never was kidnapped, I never saw you . . . (*He tenses up.*)

EXTERIOR: WOODS. DAY.

The three cops moving slowly through the woods. JABLONSKI *hand-signals them to look ahead. They look ahead.*

Angle point of view: A buck, his head down, in a thicket ahead.

Angle: The men signal HILL *to move ahead and take a shot.* HILL *moves slowly forward, starts to bring his rifle up and takes a step.* HILL *screams.*

HILL: Oh my God!!!

(*The two other men run up to him.*)

JABLONSKI: What is it . . . ???

RENKO: Bobby!!! Bobby!!! What is it???

HILL: I stepped on a . . . I stepped on a . . . I got a damn *spike* through my foot!!!

(*He continues moaning as the two men start to minister to him.*)

EXTERIOR: ROADSIDE. DAY.

GOLDBLUME, *his head down, still on the edge of the grave. Beat. He hears the sound of a car driving away. Beat. He starts to cry. He raises his head.*

Angle: GOLDBLUME *on the grave. He looks around him. He is alone. The car is gone. He slowly gets up out of the grave. He is still crying. He quiets himself. He starts back to the road. It is just dawn. Camera follows him out to the road. He sees a car coming down the road. He holds out his thumb. The car does not stop. Hold. Another car comes down the road.* GOLDBLUME *waves his arms. The car does not stop.* GOLDBLUME *hangs his head. Tries to get his breathing under control. He hears another car. Raises his head. He hunts in his pockets, holds up his shield. As the sound of the car approaches, he screams:*

GOLDBLUME: Won't somebody *help* me??? Isn't anybody going to *help* me??? I'm a *police* officer!!!

INTERIOR: RUN-DOWN CABIN. DAY.

All of the hunting paraphernalia and foodstuffs have been packed. HILL *is sitting on the table, his foot is being bandaged by* RENKO.

HILL: Hell of an ending for a weekend in the country.

RENKO: Well, these things *happen,* my boy.

HILL: Should've looked where I was going.

JABLONSKI: Can't look where you're going, look at the deer the same time . . .

HILL: Oh yeah, oh yeah, oh man, I'm going to get *tetanus,* get a "shot," walk with my *foot* in a cast for the whole time . . .

RENKO: What is life without adventure . . . ?

JABLONSKI: Come on, I want to get you to a hospital . . .

HILL: No. I'm fine, I'm fine, man, don't go make a spectacle of me . . . let's get the place straightened out, and then we'll head back to town.

(RENKO *holds up a four-inch rusty spike.*)

RENKO: I'm going to *save* this spike, Bobby Hill, get it mounted on a big plush plaque, hang in your knotty-pine den as a memento of our Hunting Trip.

JABLONSKI: And *wasn't* that buck something?

RENKO: *Had* to go six points, a hundred ninety pounds.

HILL: Hundred ninety, are you guys *nuts*? That there was a *ten* point buck, over two hundred five, two hundred ten pounds, man, I got the glass on him, he blotted out the sky . . . !

RENKO: *He's* still there, Babe. *He's* still there, next week, week after.

HILL: *When* we all going to get free time together again . . . ?

RENKO: Then we will bear him in our memory.

INTERIOR: HILL STREET SQUAD ROOM. DAY.

A hubbub at the front desk. GOLDBLUME *comes in, disheveled.*

KHAKI OFFICER: Lieutenant Goldblume, we didn't expect you 'til . . .

GOLDBLUME: Well you know, I . . . I'd like the form "carrying a back-up gun . . ." Could you please . . .

(He points toward his office, and continues there. Camera follows BATES over to him.)

BATES: Surprised to see you back, Lieutenant. Hope things went well with your secret Society of Hunters.

GOLDBLUME: Yeah, my car was stolen. I never *got* th . . .

BATES: Your *car* was stolen . . . ?

(BELKER walks outside the office. To BATES:)

BELKER: Sarge? Could I talk to you a moment. You're back early, Lieutenant? Any luck . . . ?

(BELKER and BATES walk off. GOLDBLUME fumbles his key right out of his pocket. Unlocks his desk, takes out a revolver from the desk drawer. Opens it, checks that it is unloaded. He takes out a box of shells and loads the revolver. As he is loading it the KHAKI OFFICER enters.)

KHAKI OFFICER: Form, Back-up Revolver, carrying of.

(He puts the form on the desk. GOLDBLUME finishes loading the revolver, puts it in his holster.)

GOLDBLUME: Thank you.

KHAKI OFFICER: And, sir, you will have to schedule time at the range, and qualify to . . .

GOLDBLUME: Yes, yes, let's do that right now.

KHAKI OFFICER: I can . . .

(GOLDBLUME *gets up and walks the* KHAKI OFFICER *out of his office. Camera follows* GOLDBLUME.)

GOLDBLUME: Let's do that right away, tell them I can come right down . . .

(*They go back to the front desk, passing* BUNTZ.)

BUNTZ: Get 'em already, Lieutenant. Am I going to walk out that door and see a hundred twelve pound buck strapped on the fenders of your car . . . ?

(*At the front desk, the* KHAKI OFFICER *calls the range to make an appointment for* GOLDBLUME. GOLDBLUME *looks on.*)

KHAKI OFFICER (*on phone*): . . . he's free to . . .

GOLDBLUME: I'm free right now, I can come right down and . . .

(*He hears a voice over his shoulder.*)

VOICE (*Proprietor of Currency Exchange*): They said that he was probably still in the area.

(GOLDBLUME *turns and sees the* PROPRIETOR. *Beat.*)

PROPRIETOR: They said he was probably in the area the whole time. You could of seen him on the street. (*The* PROPRIETOR *holds up the composite circular of the* ROBBER.) You could of even gotten a *look* at him.

GOLDBLUME: I didn't see *anyone* on the street.

PROPRIETOR: They said come down, look at *mug* books. I said "Yes, it's going to help you *catch* that guy, you *bet* I will, before he . . ."

GOLDBLUME: Uh-huh . . .

PROPRIETOR: Before he *kills* someone . . .

(*The* OFFICER *escorting the* PROPRIETOR *takes him by the arm.*)

OFFICER: This way, sir.

PROPRIETOR: And, you *ask* me, though you *didn't* ask me, I think that you should have stayed to *help*. (*The* PROPRIETOR *walks off.*)

KHAKI OFFICER (*to* GOLDBLUME): One thirty this afternoon. Range qualifying session.

GOLDBLUME: Thank you. (GOLDBLUME *starts to walk, somewhat shakily, back to his office. Camera follows. Over his shoulder:*) Could someone get me a form, please, for a stolen car . . .

(*Camera follows him into his office. He locks the door behind him, sits at his desk. He looks through a group of papers on his desk. Takes one out, looks at it.*)

(*Angle point of view: It is the composite drawing of the* ROBBER.)

(*Angle:* GOLDBLUME *looking at the drawing. He hears a knocking at his door. He looks up.*)

(*Angle point of view: It is Captain* FURRILLO *knocking at the door.* GOLD-BLUME *guiltily shuffles the drawing back into the stack. He goes up and opens the door.* FURRILLO *enters.*)

FURRILLO: You're back early.

GOLDBLUME: I, well, *you* know.

FURRILLO: I wanted to thank you, for giving the speech.

GOLDBLUME: Um-hmmm.

FURRILLO: I think . . . it took a little bit of *courage* to talk to those kids about some serious stuff. (*Beat.*) Are you alright?

GOLDBLUME: Up all night.

FURRILLO: Well. Thank you.

GOLDBLUME: Mmm.

(*Beat.* FURRILLO *exits.* GOLDBLUME *takes out the circular from the pile of papers.*)

(*Angle point of view: The circular.*)

(*ANGLE INTERIOR: THE SQUAD ROOM.* BATES *and* BUNTZ *jabbering.*)

BATES: . . . just a bunch of manly *nonsense,* and there's *enough* violence in the world . . .

BUNTZ: It's manly nonsense if it's not your "thing"; if not, what is this, "*Name* calling . . ."

BATES: Oh Not To The Deer! Not if the *Deer* is killed, then it's not name calling . . .

(*ANGLE INTERIOR: GOLDBLUME'S OFFICE.* GOLDBLUME, *watching* BATES *and* BUNTZ. *As their conversation takes them off screen, behind them, he sees the* PROPRIETOR *looking through the mug shots. Beat.* GOLDBLUME *gets up, holding the composite drawing. Camera follows him out of his office over to* FURRILLO'S *office. He knocks on the door.*)

FURRILLO (*through the door*): Come in.

(GOLDBLUME *enters, camera follows.* FURRILLO *looks up from his papers.*)

GOLDBLUME: I was kidnapped last night.

EXTERIOR: RUN-DOWN HUNTING SHACK. DAY.

The station wagon loaded. JABLONSKI *and* RENKO *helping the injured* HILL *to the car.*

JABLONSKI: Give one last sweep to the area, and let's head home.

(*They put* HILL *into the car, then stand and sweep the area.*)

RENKO: Didn't even fire a shot.

JABLONSKI: Well, sometimes that's the way it is.

(*Angle point of view: The orange-juice can sitting up on a stump.*)

(*Angle:* RENKO *and* JABLONSKI.)

JABLONSKI: "Leave it better than you found it."

(JABLONSKI *starts to walk toward the orange-juice can.* RENKO *motions him back behind him.* JABLONSKI *steps back behind him.* RENKO *looks at the orange-juice can for a long moment. Sweeps his hunting jacket aside, draws his revolver and fires three shots at the orange-juice can. Beat.*)
(*Angle point of view: The orange-juice can still standing.*)

(*Angle:* JABLONSKI *and* RENKO. RENKO *shrugs.* JABLONSKI *gets into the station wagon and starts it.* RENKO *walks over to the orange-juice can and puts it in his pocket.*)

We Will Take You There

Episode One:
A Hudson's Bay Start

The Lord knows what we may find, dear lass,
And the Deuce knows what we may do—
But we're back once more on the old trail,
    our own trail, the out trail,
We're down, hull-down, on the Long Trail—
    the trail that is always new.

—RUDYARD KIPLING

Dramatis Personae

DANNY ESPOSITO
MIKE ANDERTON
MACLAREN
PROFESSOR GEORGE SCHOLTZ
KAREN SCHOLTZ, HIS WIFE

PROLOGUE

A quiet side-street somewhere in small-town America. An old brickface garage, its one large door open. A postman moves past the door. A young man carrying a suitcase, a coat slung over his shoulder, moves into the frame and stands with his back to the camera. We have not seen his face. He stands for a moment outside the garage door, then enters.

Camera follows him and we see, over his shoulder, an old Land-Rover, up on blocks, covered in primer. Its hood is open and a man is working on its engine.

The first man walks to within ten feet of the Land-Rover, puts down his suitcase. Speaks to the man working on the engine.

FIRST MAN (Danny Esposito): I heard you were looking for a partner.

SECOND MAN (Mike Anderton) (still working on the engine, not looking up): Where'd you hear that?

DANNY ESPOSITO: John Malone.

MIKE ANDERTON: Where do you know John from?

ESPOSITO: From around.

ANDERTON: Do better than that.

ESPOSITO: A man introduced us some years ago.

ANDERTON: Who was that man?

ESPOSITO: That man was *you, compañero.*

(ANDERTON, *a handsome, rugged man in his early thirties, slowly raises his head from the machine. Looks at the man opposite him.*)

(*Camera angle reverse: For the first time, we see their faces.* ESPOSITO, *an athletic Latin-American man in his early thirties, smiling at* ANDERTON, *who is stunned. Beat.*)

ANDERTON: Man, I thought you were dead.

ESPOSITO: I *told* you: never believe that 'les you hear it from my own lips.

(ANDERTON *and* ESPOSITO *embrace.*)

ANDERTON: Where have you *been* . . . ?

ESPOSITO (*shrugs, smiles*): Hey, *you* know . . .

(*He steps back, looks at the Land-Rover.*)

So what is the *thing* here, what you *doing* . . . ?

(ANDERTON *steps over to a workbench, takes a brochure out of a box, hands one to* ESPOSITO.)

(*Insert: The brochure. In the manner of a travel brochure. It reads: "We will take you there." There is a picture of the fitted-out Land-Rover in front of a waterfall. The brochure is opened, the text reads: "Hunting, fishing, camping, exploration. U.S., North and South America, and abroad. If a truck can go there we will take you there. Fifteen years experience. References."*)

(*Angle:* ESPOSITO *holding the brochure. Looks up.*)

ESPOSITO: What is this, like a *taxi* service to the *wilds* . . .

ANDERTON (*smiling*): Something like that. You want to play?

ESPOSITO: I want to *play*? I'm *here*, ain't I . . . ? Just tell me where we're *going* . . .

ANDERTON (*ribbing him*): You're slowing down, Danny. You never used to *care* . . .

ESPOSITO (*holds up his hands, defending himself*): Just so I'll know what *coat* to bring . . . (*He walks over to the Land-Rover.*) Nice *truck* you got here.

(*He nods approvingly. Smiles at* ANDERTON.)

TITLE SEQUENCE:

A manila envelope. The brochure we have just seen is placed on top of it, a map is placed on top of the brochure, and an area on the map outlined in red grease pencil. The map and brochure are placed in the envelope, and a hand takes a rubber stamp, and stamps the upper left-hand corner of the manila envelope with the logo "We Will Take You There," the words in a large circle around the device of the Land-Rover.

ACT ONE

AUTUMN DAY.

The porch of an old house on a northern lake. Below the house a very large lake, an old wooden pier jutting out into the lake. ESPOSITO *perched on the porch looking out at the lake. From inside the house, the sound of a teakettle whistling.* ESPOSITO *gets up and goes inside.*

Camera follows him inside. The main room is fitted out as a turn-of-the-century hunting lodge, antlers on the wall, guns in racks, fish mounted. ESPOSITO *walks through this room into the kitchen where* MACLAREN, *a woodsman in his early sixties, is making instant coffee.*

ESPOSITO: Nice day.

MACLAREN: Nice day if it don't rain. No sugar for both, cream for one, is that right?

ESPOSITO: What'd you hear from the plane?

MACLAREN: Nothing since they left Prince Rupert.

ESPOSITO: Nothing?

MACLAREN: They ain't got a radio. Your client's coming here to look for *what* . . . ?

ESPOSITO: For lichens. For *moss.*

MACLAREN: Why?

ESPOSITO: Well, I don't *know* why. He's a professor.

MACLAREN: Of what?

ESPOSITO: Something to do with *moss. I* don't know . . . (ESPOSITO *takes the two coffees, leaves the room.*) Thank you.

MACLAREN: *Yessuh.*

(*Camera follows* ESPOSITO *back into the main room and upstairs and into a bedroom where* ANDERTON *is studying some maps he has spread out on the bed.*)

ANDERTON (*taking coffee*): Thank you.

ESPOSITO: Pleasure.

ANDERTON: Any word on their plane?

ESPOSITO: The plane has no radio. It's a nice day. If it does not rain. That's my report.

(*Sound of an airplane.*)

Aha.

(ANDERTON *and* ESPOSITO *go over to the balcony, go outside, A small ancient amphibian plane is circling, about to land on the far side of the lake.*)

ANDERTON: Well, let's go *meet* the people.

(*Camera follows the two out of the room, down the stairs, out to where their Land-Rover is sitting, outside the house. They get into the Rover, and drive it the fifty yards down to the dock.* MACLAREN *walks out and joins them as the amphibian plane glides to a stop at the dock. The pilot throws* MACLAREN *a line, and he makes the plane fast to the dock.* PROFESSOR GEORGE SCHOLTZ, *a man in his late fifties, dressed in safari clothes, a large revolver in a shoulder holster, jumps from the plane to the dock. The pilot starts handing out rifle cases to the* PROFESSOR.)

(*Angle of* ESPOSITO *and* ANDERTON *standing by the truck.*)

ESPOSITO: You said that fellow's looking for *moss* . . . ?

ANDERTON: I think that maybe he was fooling . . .

(*In the background* PROFESSOR SCHOLTZ *sees them. Greets them.*)

PROFESSOR SCHOLTZ: Mr. Anderton . . . ?

ANDERTON (*to* ESPOSITO): Excuse me.

(*He walks over to the* PROFESSOR, *extends his hand.*)

Professor *Scholtz* . . . ?

(MACLAREN *helps a woman in her forties out of the plane. She is togged in the style of her husband,* PROFESSOR SCHOLTZ. MACLAREN *walks back and, out of the side of his mouth, confabs with* ESPOSITO.)

MACLAREN: What did you say this fellow's looking for?

ESPOSITO: Moss.

MACLAREN: Carrying some heavy equipment go looking for moss.

ESPOSITO: It's wild moss.

(*In the background* ANDERTON *indicates* ESPOSITO.)

ANDERTON: And this is my partner, Danny Esposito.

(ESPOSITO *starts over toward them.*)

ESPOSITO (*to himself*): Yes sir, a nice day if it does not rain.

PROFESSOR: And this is my wife, Mrs. Scholtz. (*The* PROFESSOR *surveys the area around him.*) Lovely country.

(MACLAREN *is unloading rifle cases and video equipment from the plane.*)

ESPOSITO: Professor?

PROFESSOR: Mr. Esposito . . . ?

ESPOSITO: What are the rifles for?

PROFESSOR: They're tranquilizing guns.

ESPOSITO: For *moss* . . . ?

PROFESSOR (*looks around to his wife, on the dock*): Karen, are you okay?

MRS. SCHOLTZ: I'm fine.

(*He leads* ESPOSITO *and* ANDERTON *out of earshot of* MACLAREN, *speaks in an undertone.*)

PROFESSOR: Gentlemen, I'm sorry. I've been less than frank with you. Suffice it to say, for the moment, that the *area* of our search will remain more or less the same, but its object will be somewhat different than the one which I informed you of.

ESPOSITO: So what is it we're looking for?

PROFESSOR: When we're on the *trail,* I will, of course . . . if you will wait 'til then . . . it's a matter of security. When I tell you, you'll understand.

ESPOSITO: Oh.

(MRS. SCHOLTZ, *down on the dock, needs help with a suitcase or pack she is taking from the plane.*)

MRS. SCHOLTZ: George . . . ?

PROFESSOR: Excuse me. (*He goes down to her.*)

ESPOSITO: Wednesday is Anything Can Happen Day. (*Beat.*) What do you think?

ANDERTON (*shrugs*): Pays the piper, calls the tune.

ESPOSITO: . . . I *guess* . . .

(*They go down to the dock and start loading the Land-Rover.*)

INSIDE THE HUNTING LODGE. THE LIVING ROOM.

Hunting trophies all over. ESPOSITO, PROFESSOR, *and* MRS. SCHOLTZ *and* ANDERTON *sitting, drinking coffee.*

PROFESSOR (*holding forth*): . . . operating in the tradition of Ancient Voyagers, which is to say: each mission, each ship had a *pilot,* his responsibility was the actual day-to-day functioning of the ship; and, over him, a *Captain,* who is charged with the *direction* of the mission which is, of course, myself. (*Nods to* ANDERTON.) Now: you were saying?

ANDERTON (*stands*): Thank you. (*He picks up a small pack, marked with a large Day-Glo cross. Holds it up.*) This is a little *day*pack. What's in it? (*He starts unloading it.*) Several packets of raisins and nuts. Some chocolate. A flashlight. A small first-aid kit. A hunting knife. Some nylon line, a whistle. Matches. A small hatchet. Most importantly . . . (*He takes a compass out of a side pocket.*) A compass. (*Takes a beat. Composes his thoughts.*) We are going out into the woods. Where any of these things could save your life. Where the presence of any of them could mean the difference between life and death. Your *safety* is the responsibility of me and my partner. We are here to take you where you want to go, to help you accomplish whatever it is you want to do, to bring you back *safely.* But you're going to have to do your part. *Think. THINK BEFORE YOU ACT.* Stay with the truck. Stay in camp. Do not *leave* the camp except with Danny or myself. You may have outdoor skills. Defer to us. Let's do things *our* way. We'll make the fires and we'll dowse the fires, we'll mark the trail and we'll read the maps for you. What you're paying us for is *technique,* which is to say *habit:* the ability to act correctly faster than you can think. This is what we're trained to do. Listen to us. Use your common sense, stay alert. That's it. Tomorrow we'll be heading . . . *North?* Professor . . . ?

PROFESSOR: That is correct. North. I thank you, and so if you could show us to our rooms, I'm sure my wife . . .

ANDERTON: You want to tell them, Danny . . . ?

ESPOSITO: Thank you. (*He rises, goes to the front of the room.*) We're going to be making a Hudson's Bay Start. Let me explain that to you: The Fur Trade: the eighteenth, the nineteenth, and twentieth century, all of this area, of course, was controlled by the Hudson's Bay Company, the Fur Trade. They found that when their men went off on an expedition that they made a better start if they spent the last night before they left, not in the *camp,* but half a mile *outside* the camp. And living as they would on the trail . . .

PROFESSOR: What was the purpose of this?

ESPOSITO: To make a good start. To break camp early and get on the trail. To not waste the day looking for the articles that one has left behind, to shake down, to get in the right frame of mind. We've chosen a campsite (*points*) 'bout half a mile back in the woods, we'll get some practice pitching *camp,* we'll talk about some safety procedures, I've got some *venison* that I've bought from Mr. Maclaren, it's out of season, but he tells me it died of a broken heart. So. Let's pack up the . . .

PROFESSOR: Mrs. Scholtz and I . . .

MRS. SCHOLTZ: I'm alright, George.

PROFESSOR: I approve in the abstract of your plan . . .

ESPOSITO: Then let us be philosophers, Sir, let us live *as if* those things
of which we approved *in the abstract* were the case.

(*Sound of the airplane leaving.*)

And there goes your taxi, so we're stuck with each other awhile.
Who'd like to help me load the truck? (ESPOSITO *goes outside.*)

MRS. SCHOLTZ: I'll help.

(*The* PROFESSOR *hangs back, comes up to* ANDERTON.)

PROFESSOR: Mr. Anderton.

ANDERTON: Mike.

PROFESSOR: Mike, yes. Mike. One question. I saw the first-aid kit,
but in the event of a *medical* emergency . . .

ANDERTON: We have a fully stocked medical kit in the truck. Danny
and I are both trained in its use.

PROFESSOR: Yes, yes, but, for example, what if there was a *serious* . . .

ANDERTON: *Seriously,* my partner once removed a man's appendix with
a hunting knife.

PROFESSOR: Is that true?

ANDERTON: Yes, sir, that's absolutely true.

OUTSIDE. AT THE SIDE OF THE TRUCK.

ESPOSITO *and* MRS. SCHOLTZ *loading the Rover.*

ESPOSITO: Some fine equipment you got here, Ma'am.

MRS. SCHOLTZ: Mmm.

ESPOSITO: What's it for?

MRS. SCHOLTZ: "What's it for" is to get my husband out of the house. How old are you?

(*The* PROFESSOR *comes out of the house, comes up to* ESPOSITO.)

PROFESSOR: Mr. Esposito?

ESPOSITO: Sir?

PROFESSOR: Did you once remove a man's appendix with a hunting knife?

ESPOSITO: Yes sir. I had to. He was trying to kill me.

(ANDERTON *comes out of the house, comes over to the truck.*)

ANDERTON: Let's go camping.

(MACLAREN *comes up from the pier, calls to them.*)

MACLAREN: Looks like rain.

ESPOSITO (*under his breath, to* ANDERTON): Good "Mossing" weather.

ANDERTON: How do you like being a businessman?

ESPOSITO: Anything to get out of the house. What are we looking for?

ANDERTON: We aren't looking. He's looking. We're *driving*. You *heard* the man.

ESPOSITO (*shrugs*): Okay.

(MRS. SCHOLTZ *and her husband are in the truck.*)

All set . . . ? (*He gets into the shotgun seat.*) And away we go.

ACT TWO

THE CAMPSITE. DUSK.

Three tents, attached to the Land-Rover. A campfire in the center, the wind is starting to blow. A corner of one of the tents has come loose and is flapping. KAREN SCHOLTZ comes out of her tent and tries to fasten down the corner which has come loose. MIKE ANDERTON, holding a kerosene lantern, crossing from tent to tent, speaks to ESPOSITO, who is tending the dying fire.

ANDERTON: Danny!

ESPOSITO: Yo!

ANDERTON (*pointing to* MRS. SCHOLTZ *and the tent*): Tighten it up, will you . . . ?

(ESPOSITO *nods, goes to help* MRS. SCHOLTZ. ANDERTON *continues into the other tent.*)

ESPOSITO: I'll do that. (*He works refastening the tent.*) Blowing up a bit.

MRS. SCHOLTZ: It's beautiful out here.

ESPOSITO: It most certainly is. (*He finishes with the tent, starts back to the fire.*)

MRS. SCHOLTZ: We have any more coffee?

ESPOSITO: Uh-hmm . . .

(*He pours her some, they sit on a log by the fire. Beat.*)

MRS. SCHOLTZ: It makes you lonely sometimes. Doesn't it?

ESPOSITO: What? Being outside. Yes. I . . . I don't know . . .

MRS. SCHOLTZ: Hmm. You feel at home here.

ESPOSITO: Uh-hmm.

MRS. SCHOLTZ: That must be a very good feeling.

ESPOSITO: Well. I suppose it *is*.

MRS. SCHOLTZ: I make you nervous.

ESPOSITO (*smiles*): I think you just got to loosen up a bit. You got to leave the *city* behind. You will. In a day or two.

MRS. SCHOLTZ: I will?

ESPOSITO: Sure. I'll tell you what. Most of the time that people think: I have to do *this*, the *world* is coming to an end . . . a *business* meeting . . . what it is: it's too much *coffee* . . . not enough time to themselves. (*Beat.*) Not enough quiet.

MRS. SCHOLTZ (*bemused*): Hmmm. And that's the answer to the problems of the world.

ESPOSITO: Yes, Ma'am, that's what I think . . . two things. Now: Maybe I'm this unsophisticated guy who doesn't understand the problem . . . (*Shrugs.*) And maybe I'm *right*. (*Smiles.*) You want a donut?

(*Inside a tent. The* PROFESSOR *at a small folding table. Maps all around him. He speaks into a small tape recorder.*)

PROFESSOR: . . . north on *this* trail A-5. (*He makes notes on a scratchpad.*) To Kenyon's Hill. The basic bearing is . . . (*He hunts for something in the pile of maps on the table, he cannot find it. He spies the small daypack marked with the Day-Glo cross hanging on a peg on the tent upright, he goes into the side pocket, takes out the compass, comes back to the table.*) The basic bearing is 335 degrees. The *Lair*, according to the . . . (*He makes more notes on the scratchpad.*) According to Nessy and Mosher "Notes on Anthropoids," . . . should lie within five to six hundred yards of . . .

(ANDERTON *comes into the tent. The* PROFESSOR *stops speaking, covers his maps and notes, turns off the tape recorder.*)

Mr. Anderton . . . ?

ANDERTON: Just checking, Sir. Everything alright?

PROFESSOR: Mmm. I'm fine. Thank you. It's . . . *tomorrow* . . . we'll have breakfast at . . . ?

ANDERTON: Whenever you say, we can spend the day in *camp* if you want and set out Thurs . . .

PROFESSOR: No. We've, I want to be (*points at map*) *here* on the twenty-third. I want to set out tomorrow.

ANDERTON: Then I'd say, we'll get up early anyway. We could break camp . . . I think you'll find we can be on the road by eight. Eight thirty, no problem.

PROFESSOR: Fine. (*Sighs.*) Fine. I'm glad we were able to do this together. (*Smiles patronizingly.*) You know, it's not hard to be a *visionary*, Mr. Anderton, all you have to do is be prepared to take it in the teeth from the rest of the world until they come and catch *up* to you. (*Pause.*)

ANDERTON: S'been a long day.

PROFESSOR: Yes. It has. You and your partner seem to be very good at your job. And we appreciate that. (*Beat.*) Good night.

ANDERTON: Good night, Professor. Anything you need during the night, we'll be here.

(ANDERTON *leaves the tent. Goes over to* ESPOSITO, *who is cleaning up around the fire. Camera follows.*)

ANDERTON: How's every little thing?

ESPOSITO: Fine, hey, you never told me. This is like being a cross between a hotel and a psychiatrist.

ANDERTON: Who knew? S'we get the fire out?

ESPOSITO (*looks at the sky*): Yeah. It looks like we're 'bout to get some . . .

(*The rain starts coming down in torrents.*)

Even as he spoke. Aha!

ANDERTON: Let's check the tents.

(ANDERTON *starts making the circuit of the tents, checking the lashings. He goes to the Land-Rover and rolls up all the windows, leans inside and checks the emergency brake.*)

(ESPOSITO *at the* PROFESSOR'*s tent.*)

ESPOSITO: Looks like we're going to get some heavy rain, you'll be fine, see you in the . . .

MRS. SCHOLTZ: Where's my husband . . . ?

ESPOSITO: Over at the other t . . .

MRS. SCHOLTZ: Anyone ever tell you you're a very attractive man?

ESPOSITO: That's right, Ma'am. See you in the morning.

(*He leaves her tent, struggles through the torrential rain to the car, gets out a poncho, goes down to the other tent, where the* PROFESSOR *is poring over his notes.*)

Professor, your wife's looking for you. Poncho. (*Hands him the poncho.*) Stay dry. Good night.

(ESPOSITO *leaves. The* PROFESSOR *looks down at his notes. Takes off his glasses, wipes his eyes, arranges his notes. Weights them down, puts a note up on a small portable bulletin board. Crumples some of the notes he has been taking, stands up, starts to leave the tent. He absently picks up the notes he has crumpled, looks around. Picks up an empty tin can they have been using as an ashtray, puts the crumpled notes into it, lights a match to it, puts it on the ground.* ESPOSITO *puts his head back in the tent.*)

Really blowing up!

PROFESSOR: Yes. I'll be right there.

(ESPOSITO *nods. Camera follows him through the rain, back to the front seat of the Land-Rover, where* ANDERTON *is sitting, wearing glasses, studying a map by a navigator light on the dash.*)

ESPOSITO: Nice day if it doesn't rain.

ANDERTON: Hey, what are you, a weatherman?

ESPOSITO: No, a weatherman is "fifty percent *chance* it doesn't rain." "Nice *day* if it doesn't rain" is a philosopher. You got a route for tomorrow . . . ?

ANDERTON: Uh-hmm.

ESPOSITO: Where we going . . . ?

(ANDERTON *points out the route on the map.*)

ANDERTON: By the *truck* to *here* . . .

ESPOSITO: We'll camp there tomor . . . (*Sees something through the windshield.*) And there he goes: The Man in *Style* is the Man who can Smile!

(*Through the windshield we see the* PROFESSOR *hurrying through the rain back to his tent.*)

ANDERTON: Forgot his poncho.

ESPOSITO: *There* goes a man who is *wet*.

ANDERTON: The wife and them all snug in their tents?

ESPOSITO: Yup. Bugs in rugs. Well, one bug in a rug, anyway.

ANDERTON: Yeah? Tell me.

ESPOSITO: Broad's got roving eyes and toys in the attic, a bad combination.

ANDERTON: So it goes. The truck to *there* (*pointing at the map*), camp there, three, four o'clock 'morrow afternoon, and I think Friday we'll take him out on foot.

ESPOSITO: What do you think my man's *looking* for?

ANDERTON (*shakes his head*): I do not *know* . . . (*Puts away the map.*) That's enough for one day. You want a drink?

ESPOSITO: *Yeah,* I want a drink. We allowed to drink on duty?

ANDERTON: This day's *over,* Dan. I'm punching out.

(*He goes back into the body of the Rover, opens a compartment, brings out a bottle of bourbon and two glasses. He pours and he and* ESPOSITO *sit listening to the rain. Beat.*)

ESPOSITO: Ain't this nice . . . ?

(ANDERTON *nods. Beat. Through the windshield we see the tent the* PRO-FESSOR *has been in burst into flame.*)

Oh, God.

(*Angle: Outside the Land-Rover.* ESPOSITO *and* ANDERTON *burst out of the truck. Run to the back and take out a fire extinguisher. Rush to the burning tent and start cutting it down. The* PROFESSOR *and his wife come out of their tent.* ANDERTON *runs by them holding the fire extinguisher.*)

ANDERTON: It's alright. It's alright. *Stay in your tent!* It's alright!

(ANDERTON *rushes on. Starts spraying the tent with the fire extinguisher. The* PROFESSOR *rushes to the tent, starts to rush inside.*)

ANDERTON: Danny!

(ESPOSITO *turns, sees the* PROFESSOR, *restrains him.*)

PROFESSOR: My map! My map!

ESPOSITO: Wha . . . ?

PROFESSOR: My *maps* . . . my maps are in the . . .

ANDERTON (*above them*): Let it burn . . . Let'em burn!!!

PROFESSOR: My maps are in the . . . (*He tries to push past* ESPOSITO.)

ESPOSITO: Mike! *Take* 'em!

(ESPOSITO *goes into the flaming tent, starts throwing stuff out of it.* ANDERTON *restrains the* PROFESSOR. *Hold. Throws him away from the flames and to the ground, goes into the tent after* ESPOSITO *and drags him out.*)

ANDERTON: Are you nuts!!!??? Let's get this thing out.

(*The area outside the tent is strewn with the* PROFESSOR'*s papers,* ANDERTON *and* ESPOSITO *work at getting the fire out, the* PROFESSOR *scavenges on the ground for his paper.*)

PROFESSOR (*to himself*): Where is it . . . ? Where is it . . . ? (*He spies something ten yards away from him.*)

(*Angle point of view: His map.*)

(*Angle: He starts after it, it blows away. He starts into the woods in pursuit of it, which carries him past* ANDERTON *and* ESPOSITO, *who are just bringing the fire into control. They do so, and retire, to watch it smolder.*)

ANDERTON: You okay . . . ?

ESPOSITO (*simultaneously*): You okay . . . ?

ANDERTON: I'm fine.

(ESPOSITO *starts picking up the papers that are not blown by the wind. He weights them down with the emergency pack. He looks around.* MRS. SCHOLTZ *is huddled in the front of her tent.* ANDERTON *goes over to her.*)

It's fine. It's under control. You'll be fine. Stay dry, stay in your tent. Danny's got most of the stuff out of the . . .

MRS. SCHOLTZ: Where's my husband?

ANDERTON: He . . . ? (*He looks around.*)

(*Angle point of view:* ESPOSITO *picking up the papers, stashes them in safety in the front of the Rover.*)

(*Angle:* ANDERTON *goes over to him.*)

ANDERTON: Where's the professor?

(*Beat.* ESPOSITO *looks around. They split up and make a circuit of the camp. They meet back by the truck.* ANDERTON *gives* ESPOSITO *a quick questioning look.* ESPOSITO *shakes his head "No."*)

ESPOSITO: You want to stay or go?

ANDERTON: I'll go.

(ESPOSITO *throws him the emergency pack which he has just taken out of the burning tent.* ANDERTON *takes out the flashlight, shines it, the beam is strong.*)

ESPOSITO: He went North. (ESPOSITO *points.*) You're heading three-forty degrees.

ANDERTON: You sure?

ESPOSITO: That's how I parked the truck.

(ANDERTON *looks down at his watch, shining the flashlight on it.*)

(*Angle: The watch. It is 9:30.*)

(*Angle:* ANDERTON *and* ESPOSITO.)

ANDERTON: *See* you . . .

(ANDERTON *heads out into the woods along the path* ESPOSITO *has pointed.* ESPOSITO *goes into the truck. Turns it on, turns on the headlights. He beeps the horn several times. Gets out of the cab, comes over to* MRS. SCHOLTZ.)

ESPOSITO: Can you hear that?

MRS. SCHOLTZ: What?

ESPOSITO: The *horn.* The *truck* horn. Can you hear it?

MRS. SCHOLTZ: Where's my husband?

ESPOSITO: Ma'am, he's in the woods. Can you hear the horn?

MRS. SCHOLTZ: He's in the woods?

ESPOSITO: Mike will bring him back.

MRS. SCHOLTZ (*distraught, sarcastic*): Oh, "Mike." "Mike." "Mike will bring him back."

ESPOSITO: Yes, Ma'am.

MRS. SCHOLTZ: Or what? Or What? Or "die trying"?

ESPOSITO: Ma'am, that will not be necessary, but the answer is: Yes, Mike will bring him back or he will die trying. I'm going to honk the horn. You tell me if you can hear it.

(ESPOSITO *goes back into the Rover. Honks the horn every three seconds. He turns on the windshield wipers. We see* MRS. SCHOLTZ *standing forlornly in front of her tent.*)

ACT THREE

INSIDE THE TENT.

Close up: A game of solitaire laid out, a woman's hand sweeping up the cards.

Angle: ESPOSITO *and* MRS. SCHOLTZ *sitting at the folding table. Beat.*

ESPOSITO: You know *casino?*

(*Beat. He looks down at his watch.*)

(*Insert: The watch. It is ten minutes to twelve.*)

(*Angle:* MRS. SCHOLTZ *and* ESPOSITO.)

MRS. SCHOLTZ: Do you know there's nothing people can say about themselves that hasn't been said?

ESPOSITO: Well, people talk about themselves, what does it mean?

MRS. SCHOLTZ: What *does* it mean?

ESPOSITO: They're try'n to choose up sides, they're try'n to create a role. We all like to be comfortable. You get into a new situation, you want people to know what that role *is*. Nothing to it.

MRS. SCHOLTZ: Do you ever have fantasies?

ESPOSITO: Everyone has fantasies.

MRS. SCHOLTZ: They do?

ESPOSITO: Yes.

MRS. SCHOLTZ: Do you?

ESPOSITO: Sure. Let me tell you something, nice thing about them is you don't have to *act* on them.

MRS. SCHOLTZ: Come sit by me. I'm frightened.

ESPOSITO: Come *on*. *Look:* hey?

(*He goes to the front of the tent, opens the flap, looks out.*)

Do you mind if I *talk* to you . . . ? You, you know. People are *out* there. Your husband is out there. My partner is out there. Someone you're close to goes through something. *Whatever.* One person: "How can I help." "I hope that they are alright." Another person, *here:* "My, *this* is out there, my *husband* . . . I don't need him." Huh. "I never liked him *anyway.* Far from I want him to be safe, I hope he never comes back. I can live my fantasy. *I* know! This *Guy* I never met. He's an attractive man . . . ! I'll bet he'll understand me. Or could please me or something . . . how" . . . am I, uh, upsetting you . . . ? "How wonderful I'm so free at this moment I can live my *own* life. I'm unbound by all the middle-class *nonsense* that makes everyone else so dull. 'Cause I don't need him anyhow."

MRS. SCHOLTZ: Oh and is *that* the world that you see . . . ?

ESPOSITO: Yes. I'm going to the truck.

MRS. SCHOLTZ: Can I come with you . . . ?

ESPOSITO: You want to come with me?

MRS. SCHOLTZ: Yes.

ESPOSITO: Sure. (*Sighs.*) Come on, let's beep the horn.

(*He opens the flap of the tent. We see the storm again. Over his shoulder:*)

Put on your poncho.

DEEP IN THE WOODS. DARK.

The rain pounding. ANDERTON *stopping to examine the ground. Shines his light on the earth. Straightens, checks his watch, moves his eyes slowly to right and left in half circle, moves on, surveys the ground again with flashlight. Moves on. Stoops, surveys the ground again. He retraces his steps and goes back to the last sure track. He moves from there out to his left, and repeats the procedure. He moves on.*

Back in the cab of the truck, ESPOSITO *and* MRS. SCHOLTZ. *She is smoking a cigarette. Stubs it out, takes out a cigarette pack.*

MRS. SCHOLTZ: You want one?

ESPOSITO: Gave it up.

(*Beat.*)

MRS. SCHOLTZ: Long ago?

ESPOSITO: Un-hmmm. (*Beat.*)

MRS. SCHOLTZ: You want one anyway?

ESPOSITO: No thanks.

MRS. SCHOLTZ: Are they alright out there?

ESPOSITO: I think that they . . . I don't know. I, *finally* all it is, is it's *wet*. If your husband stays *calm* till Mike finds him, he'll be fine.

MRS. SCHOLTZ: Mike will find him?

ESPOSITO: Yes. Eventually. I'd say probably quickly.

MRS. SCHOLTZ: He won't get lost?

ESPOSITO: *Mike?* (*Smiles.*) No. I don't think so. That's his business.

MRS. SCHOLTZ: Have you ever been lost?

ESPOSITO: As Daniel Boone said, they asked him if he'd ever been lost, he said, no, he'd never been lost, but once he was a tad *bewildered* for five days . . . (*Smiles. Beat.*)

Mrs. Scholtz: Are you mad at me?

Esposito: *Mad* at you? No, I'm not mad at you at all. I kind of *like* you . . .

Mrs. Scholtz: You do?

Esposito: Yeah.

Mrs. Scholtz: *Why?*

Esposito: Well . . . *why.* Well, here's two possibilities: One: I'm not very perceptive, and I'm taken in by your essentially bitchy facade, and *two,* is that you're basically a likable person. (*Beat.*) You want to listen to the radio? (*Beat.*)

Mrs. Scholtz: Sure.

Esposito: Let's see what we can get.

(*He turns on the radio. We hear old-time dance music. He tries the windshield wipers for a moment, nothing to be seen. He turns them off. He looks at his watch.*)

(*Insert: It is 1:20.*)

(*Angle:* Esposito. *He begins to look worried.*)

IN THE WOODS.

Anderton *stooping. Examining the tracks. Straightens, is about to shine his light. Stops. Looks* intently *into the woods before him. He moves ahead hurriedly. Lightning flashes, we see the* PROFESSOR *stumbling blindly about in the woods. He is disoriented.* ANDERTON *moves up to him, moves around before him, approaches him.*

ANDERTON: Professor!

(*The* PROFESSOR *is frightened. Starts to bolt away from* ANDERTON. ANDERTON *runs after him. Tackles him. The* PROFESSOR *tries to struggle up and away.*)

ANDERTON: It's alright. It's alright. It's *me* . . . it's Anderton. It's alright . . . You're *fine* . . . It's *alright* . . .

(*The* PROFESSOR *comes to his senses.*)

PROFESSOR: You . . .

ANDERTON: It's alright.

PROFESSOR: You . . .

ANDERTON: It's alright. You're fine. You're fine. Everything is fine. We're going *back* now. (*Beat.*) We're going back now. Now we're just going to be *still* for a moment, now.

(*He stands with his arm on the* PROFESSOR*'s shoulder, calming him.*)

PROFESSOR (*Still very disoriented, and very weak*): I . . . I . . . I . . .

ANDERTON: You're fine. Can you walk?

PROFESSOR: I'm so tired.

ANDERTON: Okay. Here's what we're going to . . .

(*He leads the* PROFESSOR *to the lee of a large tree, sits him down, squats by him.*)

You stay here . . .

(*He has second thoughts, as the* PROFESSOR *starts to fidget, still disoriented.*)

You got a dollar bill . . . you got a dollar bill . . . ?

PROFESSOR: I . . .

ANDERTON: I need it and we have to have it. Now. You have a dol . . .

PROFESSOR: Yes. I . . . I think . . . (*He rummages in his pocket, takes out a moneyclip, takes out a dollar bill, holds it limply.*)

ANDERTON: Look:

(*Takes a small pocketknife from his own pocket, hands it to the* PROFESSOR, *takes a coil of nylon rope from his emergency pack, cuts off four or five feet, and hands the knife, the rope, and the dollar to the* PROFESSOR.)

We need six-inch lengths . . . are you listening to me. Listen to me: we need this: we need it now: six . . . You need to cut this line into six-inch lengths. You got it. Are you listening to me. Wake *up* now. I need this rope cut into the lengths of this dollar bill . . .

PROFESSOR: You want me to cut the rope . . . ?

ANDERTON: I want you to cut it *exactly*. It must be *exactly*. In the length of this dollar bill. You got it?

PROFESSOR: How many . . .

ANDERTON: As many as you can. You with me?

PROFESSOR: I . . .

ANDERTON: You with me?

PROFESSOR: Yes.

ANDERTON: Good. You're doing fine. Good.

(*The* PROFESSOR *starts cutting the nylon line into lengths, measuring it against the dollar bill.* ANDERTON *takes a small hatchet out of his emergency pack. Camera follows him as he cuts down several small one-inch diameter saplings to a length of about five feet. He strips them, looking back every once in a while at the* PROFESSOR *to check on him. When he has six or eight saplings he carries them back to the* PROFESSOR, *who is finishing cutting the lengths of rope.*)

ANDERTON: How we doing?

PROFESSOR: Yes. I have it.

ANDERTON: Good. Keep it up.

(ANDERTON *takes the rope lengths the* PROFESSOR *has cut, and lashes the saplings together into a 5x5 frame, notching them where they join with the* PROFESSOR's *survival knife and lashing with the rope. He lashes two uprights to make a lean-to, takes several more lengths from the* PROFESSOR *and, removing his poncho, lashes it over the frame. It is now a waterproof covering.* ANDERTON *digs the ends of the lean-to and the upright into the ground, and they now have a waterproof shelter. He points the* PROFESSOR *to go beneath the lean-to.*)

PROFESSOR: What are we going to do?

ANDERTON: We're going to get dry for a while, rest up, take a little nap.

PROFESSOR: We're going to stay here tonight?

ANDERTON: You go to sleep, everything is fine.

PROFESSOR: How are we going to make a fire?

ANDERTON: That's what you're paying me for. You go to sleep.

PROFESSOR: I . . .

ANDERTON: I know.

PROFESSOR: I'm so tired.

ANDERTON: I know that you are. You go to sleep.

PROFESSOR: I lost the map.

ANDERTON: What?

PROFESSOR: I lost the map. I lost it.

ANDERTON: You go to sleep. (ANDERTON *takes off his pack, shelters it beneath the lean-to.*) You . . . you watch this stuff. Make sure nothing happens to it. I'm going to be right outside a while. You guard the stuff.

PROFESSOR: I will.

ANDERTON: What?

PROFESSOR: I will.

ANDERTON: I'm counting on you. Good.

(ANDERTON *goes out into the rain with the hatchet. He looks back on the* PROFESSOR, *who is curling up on top of the pack.* ANDERTON *starts to work cutting down some more saplings. Takes some deadwood off the ground, carries it and the saplings back to the shade of the lean-to, starts stripping the saplings, digging into the deadwood to find some dry pith, sets about building the fire.*)

PROFESSOR: I lost my map . . . I've ruined my *project* I . . .

ANDERTON: Nothing to do about it tonight. (*Listens intently.*) Rain's dying. It'll let up before the morning. They'll be coming for us soon, so you must be quiet now: I have to listen for them. You understand? (*Beat.*)

PROFESSOR: Yes.

ANDERTON: Alright, you go to sleep. Good.

(*Beat. He puts a match to the fire he has been building, it takes the match and starts, he shelters it, adds small pieces of kindling, builds up the fire.*)

AT THE TRUCK.

MRS. SCHOLTZ, *asleep on* ESPOSITO's *shoulder.* ESPOSITO *turns on the windshield wipers. Nothing. Rubs his eyes, turns off the radio which is playing very softly, a symphony. He rotates his neck to get a kink out. Slowly, so as not to disturb* MRS. SCHOLTZ, *sinks down slightly in his seat, and closes his eyes.*

ACT FOUR

THE LEAN-TO IN THE WOODS. MORNING.

ANDERTON *has built a large campfire some yards from the lean-to. He has constructed a drying rack over it and is drying out his clothes. He is stripped naked squatting before the fire, looking at the* PROFESSOR. ANDERTON *squints at the sun, looks at the* PROFESSOR, *picks up a small pebble, and flips it at the sleeping* PROFESSOR. *He does it again. The* PROFESSOR *wakes up.*

PROFESSOR: Where are we?

ANDERTON: Like that old joke, "we're in the woods," you ever want to be an Indian?

(*The* PROFESSOR *gets up, wet, sleepy, miserable.*)

PROFESSOR: Where are we?

ANDERTON: I *surmise*—(*of his clothes*) Take that stuff off and dry it off—come on, there's nobody here but us chickens. I surmise we're three-four hours from the truck, which is basically south.

PROFESSOR: *Basically* south . . .

ANDERTON: I have a *confession* to make which is that my highline Emergency Survival Pack seems to be without a compass. (*Beat.*) You have one?

PROFESSOR: No, but they'll be coming for us.

ANDERTON: No, they won't. Danny will stay with the truck.

PROFESSOR: You said they'll be coming for us.

ANDERTON: No. Just trying to put your mind at rest. They couldn't find us. Grace of God, I found *you*, 'cause the rain was washing out the track.

PROFESSOR: They *aren't* coming for us?

ANDERTON: No. We're going to dry off, and then we're going to walk out.

PROFESSOR: How will we walk out without a compass?

ANDERTON: What direction were we going in the truck?

PROFESSOR: I . . . North.

ANDERTON: The road was going North?

PROFESSOR: Yes.

ANDERTON: Last night we walked basically North. Did we cross the road?

PROFESSOR: No.

ANDERTON: Then, since we were camped to the left of the road and walked North, if we head due East we'll intersect the road. We then make a right turn and walk back to camp. (*Beat.*) *You* would have figured that out.

PROFESSOR: How do we find the East? The *sun* rises in the East!

ANDERTON: Unfailingly.

(*The* PROFESSOR *looks up, it is a completely hazy day. He cannot make out the sun.*)

PROFESSOR: But we can't see the sun today.

ANDERTON: That's right.

PROFESSOR: So how can we find the East?

ANDERTON: What do you think?

PROFESSOR: Something about the Moss on Trees . . . ?

ANDERTON: The Moss on Trees. Exactly.

PROFESSOR: It grows heavier on one side of the tree.

ANDERTON: On which side?

PROFESSOR: I don't know.

ANDERTON: Well, let's be logical.

PROFESSOR: On the . . . on the side with least sun . . . ?

ANDERTON: And which side would that be?

PROFESSOR: The *North*.

ANDERTON: *Sounds logical.* And so which way is East?

(*The* PROFESSOR *looks around, examines a tree or two, points.* ANDERTON *starts disassembling the lean-to as he speaks to the* PROFESSOR.)

That's right, the way you follow a course in the woods is you *sight*. You find your direction of travel—in this case the *East* . . . (*he points*) and you sight on an *object* . . . that gnarled tree there, for example . . .

(*He throws a packet of nuts to the* PROFESSOR.)

Have some breakfast. You walk to that object, and you *sight again*. This method brings you home. You want to take a walk.

BACK AT CAMP.

ESPOSITO *and* MRS. SCHOLTZ, *seated on a bumper of the truck, drinking coffee, chatting.*

Insert: Watch. Ten o'clock.

MRS. SCHOLTZ: You think that they're alright?

ESPOSITO: Yes, I do.

MRS. SCHOLTZ: Isn't there something we should do?

ESPOSITO: If they're not back in an hour, we will.

MRS. SCHOLTZ: What will we do?

ESPOSITO: We'll get Maclaren to get on the radio, we'll organize a search.

MRS. SCHOLTZ: My husband and I . . .

ESPOSITO: Hey, look, if you love the guy, be married to him. He's not a bad guy. Not, cut him loose, so *be* it. Everything has its down side. Huh? So, he's *arrogant*—other hand, he's a *dreamer.* He wants to go find this *thing.* I don't know, there's something marvelous in that. The whole *thing* is, why look for something *better* all the time? Why did you marry him?

MRS. SCHOLTZ: I liked him.

ESPOSITO: So *like* him.

ON THE ROAD.

The PROFESSOR *and* ANDERTON *walking, briskly.*

PROFESSOR: The technical name, actually, is the Sasquatch.

ANDERTON: Sasquatch.

PROFESSOR: In the Himalayas, the "Yeti," or, popularly, "the Abominable Snowman," though, this is, of course, a corruption.

ANDERTON: Of what?

PROFESSOR: Correctly translated, it would be "Bear-Man," in the Rocky Mountains, and, you might think, *curiously,* in the *Everglades* . . . "Big Foot."

ANDERTON: They've got 'em in the Everglades . . . ?

PROFESSOR: The range of the creature is throughout, on this continent throughout *most* wilderness regions.

ANDERTON: And how accurate are the reports of . . .

PROFESSOR: Does the creature actually exist? Yes. It exists. If you ask men in Nepal what wildlife they have on the mountains they will say Goat, Bear, Mink, Deer, *Yeti,* it's a matter of course. It exists. Why has it not been authenticated? (*Shrugs.*) People thought the Giant Squid was a figment of mapmakers' imaginations until one was found washed ashore in 1823. The *giraffe* was thought a hoax in Europe until one was brought back and exhibited in 1790. The planet *Pluto* was not discovered until 1930. It was there all the time. These creatures exist. *Films* exist, footprints exist. They are reported many times a month. The *Grizzly* bear needs five times the square miles of the Sasquatch, yet they are seen less frequently. The creature exists. I had a map of the last and largest sighting. The map was purchased from . . . the expedition has been sworn to silence, to *protect* the creature—I managed to buy the map. (*Shrugs.*) The map was going to rescue my career.

ANDERTON: Your career needs rescue?

(*We hear, faintly, a car horn beeping every three seconds.*)

Great, there go the batteries.

(*In the camp,* MRS. SCHOLTZ *at the car, beeping the horn.* ANDERTON *and the* PROFESSOR *walk into the camp. She runs up and starts embracing her husband.* ANDERTON *walks over to* ESPOSITO, *who comes out of the tent to meet him.*)

ESPOSITO: How you doing?

ANDERTON: No compass in the emergency pack.

ESPOSITO: No, huh?

ANDERTON: I didn't check it before I went out. (*Beat.*)

ESPOSITO: Never too old to learn.

ANDERTON: You know what the thing was? The Professor had a map of the Abominable Snowman.

ESPOSITO: I know. His wife told me.

ANDERTON: She did?

ESPOSITO: Yeah. We've gotten to be very close. (*Beat.*)

ANDERTON (*shakes his head*): God, it would have been great trying to track that guy.

ESPOSITO: The snowman . . . ? Well, don't give up yet, 'cause I found the map yesterday. (*He displays the map.*)

ANDERTON: You *found* it . . .

ESPOSITO: Yeah, I found it on the ground.

(ANDERTON *takes the map. Turns to look for the* PROFESSOR.)

(*Angle point of view: The* PROFESSOR *and his* WIFE *embracing.*)

(*Angle:* ESPOSITO *and* ANDERTON.)

ANDERTON: Ah, we'll do the map later.

ESPOSITO: There is a guy with his priorities straight.

(*They stroll over to the truck.* ESPOSITO *looking at the photo of the Snowman.*)

ESPOSITO: You think this turkey exists?

ANDERTON: Well, Dan, many people doubted the existence of the planet *Pluto,* 'til its discovery in 1930.

ESPOSITO: That's true. How'd you get back 'thout your compass?

ANDERTON: Moss on the trees, my friend. Like the Professor said. Our Old Friend. The Moss on Trees.

EPILOGUE

Insert: A large sheet of paper. A tracing of the foot of the Sasquatch, eighteen inches long. The paper is replaced with another, a photo of the creature. It is

*replaced with another, a comparative drawing of the Sasquatch and a man.
The Sasquatch towers over the man.*

Angle: ESPOSITO *looking at the drawing. The* PROFESSOR, *behind him, at
the truck, slinging his pack up onto the tailgate. The camp is struck.*

PROFESSOR: Alright: Karen! Let's get *with* it! Mike?!

(*Angle:* ANDERTON, *walking around the now-cleared campsite.*)

ANDERTON: Professor?

PROFESSOR: Ready?

ANDERTON: Yep.

(*The* PROFESSOR *helps his wife up into the Rover.* ESPOSITO *gets in beside her
and they sit in the back.* ANDERTON *and the* PROFESSOR *get into the driver's
seat and shotgun.*)

INSIDE THE TRUCK.

ESPOSITO: How are you today?

MRS. SCHOLTZ: Never been better.

ESPOSITO: Glad to hear it.

ANDERTON (*over his shoulder*): You bring your toothbrush?

ESPOSITO: Yeah, you remember to pack the sandwiches?

ANDERTON: Yeah. Did you turn off the iron?

ESPOSITO: Yeah.

ANDERTON: That's it, then.

MRS. SCHOLTZ: Lovely weather.

ESPOSITO: "It's always lovely Weather when Good Friends Get To-gether" (*Under his breath to* ANDERTON:) . . . to go looking for the Abominable Snowman.

PROFESSOR (*jocular*): No need to be frightened, Mr. Esposito.

ESPOSITO: Man, I grew up Sixty-third and Stony in Chicago, I'm not frightened, I'm just *interested. Hit* it, Mike.

(ANDERTON *starts the car.*)

ESPOSITO (*in the style of a TV pitchman*): And it's juuuussst that easy!

(*The truck drives off.*)